THE SHAPIRO FAMILY,
JEWISH CREATIVITY AND COURAGE IN
RUSSIA AND EASTERN EUROPE

THE SHAPIRO FAMILY, JEWISH CREATIVITY AND COURAGE IN RUSSIA AND EASTERN EUROPE

RACHEL BAYVEL

VALLENTINE MITCHELL
LONDON • CHICAGO

First published in 2024 by Vallentine Mitchell

Catalyst House,
720 Centennial Court,
Centennial Park, Elstree WD6 3SY, UK

814 N. Franklin Street,
Chicago, Illinois,
IL 60610 USA

www.vmbooks.com

British Library Cataloguing in Publication Data:
An entry can be found on request

ISBN 978 1 80371 035 8 (Paper)
ISBN 978 1 80371 036 5 (Ebook)

Library of Congress Cataloging in Publication Data:
An entry can be found on request

Contents

This is grouped in three sections: aspects of family history of the notable personalities of the Shapiro family from 11th to 20th century; more detailed family history in Russia pre-war, during and post-war in the context of key historical events over the last 80 years which the author has lived through or witnessed; articles on eminent Jewish painters in the USSR.

(Shapiro is variously written as Shapira, שפירא, Spiro, Spira, Szpira, Szapira, Schapiro, all versions are iterations of the German city of Speyer or Spira, the origin of the name).

Acknowledgements

A number of people generously helped and supported Rachel in her work. They included the former Heads of the Department of Jewish Studies at UCL: the late Professors Chimen Abramsky, John D. Klier, and Ada Rapoport-Albert. Rachel received much invaluable advice from the then UNESCO Professor of Jewish Studies at the University of Birmingham, Jonathan Webber, lately at the Jagiellonian University in Krakow, Poland, as well as its leading scholars, Prof A. K. Link-Lenczowski and Prof Michał Galas. Dr Wojciech Kulisiewicz (Director of the Library of the Polish Sejm) is thanked for providing access to the documents kept in the Archive of the Sejm and other Polish archives. Huge gratitude is owed to the internationally leading bibliographer, Brad Sabin Hill (formerly Head of the Hebrew Section of the British Library, Librarian and Fellow in Hebrew Bibliography at the Oxford Centre for Hebrew and Jewish Studies, and Dean of the Library and Senior Research Librarian at the YIVO Institute, USA) for help with many aspects of the Slavuta printing research.

Thanks are also due to Rabbi T. Loewenthal (Institute of Jewish Studies, UCL), Ilana Tahan (the British Library), and Dr Z. Jagodzinski (for many years Head of the Polish Library, London) for their kind help and assistance. All translations of Chava Shapiro's diary and letters are from Naomi Caruso's MA Thesis (McGill University, Montreal 1991), whose kind permission to use them is gratefully acknowledged. Thanks are due to Boris Ben Ari (London) and Gideon Bolotowsky (Helsinki) for valuable information about the participation of the Finnish Jewish soldiers in the Second World War.

During the 2020-21 Covid 19 lockdown, following his cancelled Bar Mitzvah celebrations, her younger grandson Pinchas (Peter) Bayvel-Zayats diligently wrote to all publishers of the different journals requesting permissions for publication of these articles in this book and helping in the editing the files. Her elder grandson Shmuel (Daniel Samuel) assisted with technical help in extracting the files.

We are grateful to the support received from our publishers Vallentine Mitchell, especially the guidance from Toby Harris, Sue Garfield and Jenny Tinson.

We also thank Sharon Mintz (Sotheby's), William Gross and Brad Sabin Hill for provision of images of books printed in Slavuta (on the cover and included in the plates of illustrations).

Rachel Bayvel (1936 – 2016): the life and background, from Leningrad to London

This book is a collection of articles written by Rachel Bayvel (née Shapiro) printed in different publications from the period during 2009 – 2011 in the UK, USA and Poland. Rachel Bayvel died in 2016 and these articles were collected by her husband, daughter and grandchildren, whose goal is to perpetuate the memory of their wife, mother and grandmother. To understand why the context of these articles could be of interest to a wide circle of readers, it is important to learn the story about the writer's background and history.

Rachel Bayvel was born in the USSR in 1936, in a city which was called Leningrad – now St Petersburg. Her parents, Shmuel and Sheindl Shapiro, came to Leningrad from shtetls (small towns) in Ukraine. The difference of this family, however, was that unlike the majority of the Jewish population in the Soviet Union, they were very religious and maintained a Jewish way of life, in spite of tremendous difficulties of doing so. From a young age, Rachel's parents explained to her that she is a descendant of a famous family, she must know her background and where she came from, and that it was her duty to follow the special customs and traditions of her ancestors – which she did, bringing up her daughter in the same way. Rachel grew up in Leningrad, the cultural capital of the USSR, and lived in the centre of this remarkable city, practically on the doorstep of the best theatres, museums and concert halls. It was a rare case in the Soviet Union to be religious and observant and simultaneously have a certain level of education. Rachel had a Masters degree from the Institute of Design and Technology and a deep knowledge of the different aspects of art. In 1962 she married Leopold Bayvel, a physicist and an academic.

Their daughter, Polina, was born in 1966 and in 1978 the family emigrated to London. Rachel started to work in the Design Department at the Head Office of M&S where she spent many years. However, all her life, it was her ambition to become a historian, and to explore her family's past. This became possible after her retirement in 2000, when she became an independent researcher. In her research, she received much encouragement and support from well-known scholars, in the UK as well as USA, Israel, and Poland. Her research focused mainly towards three areas, namely, (i) the history of her family, (ii) personal recollections about life in the Soviet Union during World War II and in Stalin's time and (iii) Soviet Jewish artists. At first, she concentrated on the life and activities of her ancestors, the famous Jewish printers, Shapiro, who founded the renowned printing press in Slavuta (also written as Slovuta, Slovita, Slawuta, סלאוויטא), Ukraine. The books printed in the Slavita printing press are considered to have special sanctity (נודעת קדושה מיוחדת) in that even the printing tools and letters were dipped in the mikvah (ritual bath) before the work began. It is thought by tzaddikim and hasidim that keeping books from the Slavuta printers has the power to protect the home and bring luck (סגולה לשמירת הבית ולהצלחה). Shapiro-printed books command high prices when they come up at auctions, and couple of examples are included here from a recent Sotheby's auction. A rare siddur (see Plate) *Seder avodah u-moreh derekh*, includes material from various Hasidic works. *Seder avodah u-moreh derekh* takes its name from the idea that Jewish prayer is a form of divine worship akin to the service (*avodah*) in the Temple (*Ta'anit* 2a). The work was also meant to serve as a guide (*moreh derekh*) to those seeking to know the laws and customs associated with prayer and to pray with gusto and proper intention. Another, siddur *Seder tefillat nehora,* a kabbalistically-tinged prayer book, was first printed in 1811, with commentary anthologized from numerous sources, appearing under the title *Seder tefillat nehora ha-shalem*, after 1819, in either general Ashkenazic (*minhag ashkenaz*) or Hasidic (*minhag sefard*) versions. Another Plate shows a rare copy of the former, issued only a short time before the Shapiro press in Slavuta ceased operations in 1836. Rachel found new materials based on which she reconstructed the history of the printing house from the end of the 18th century. She fulfilled her ambition – to piece together the history of her family. One of her main goals was to let her grandchildren know of the family they came from.

Baal Shem Tov (Besht), the founder of Hasidim, once said that the Shapiro family is one of three families, most ancient and distinguished in their ancestry. Rachel describes the history of her family in several publications (USA, UK, Poland) from the 11th century (the time of the Crusades) to 20th century. This family gave the Jewish world such luminaries as Rabbi Natan Spiro (1585-1633) from Krakow, the author of famous book *Megalleh Amukkot*, published posthumously in 1636-1639 and Rabbi Meir Shapiro (1887-1933), the founder of Daf Yomi – the page-a-day Talmud study programme. In the process of her research, Rachel had the opportunity to collaborate with the Department of Jewish Studies of the Jagellonian University in Krakow and gained access to documents from the library of the Polish Sejm (Warsaw) and other Polish archives. The study of these documents allowed to correct several erroneous statements and obtain new, previously unknown, facts concerning the life of Meir Shapiro. A chapter is dedicated to another member of the Shapiro family – Chava Shapiro (1878-1943) – who also came from Slavuta and became one of the first woman in the history of Hebrew literature. The life of Chava Shapiro is relatively unknown to the wider public and awaits to be described in a novel.

The study of the Shapiro family history required a thorough knowledge of Polish, Czech, French, German, Russian and Ukrainian languages, as well as Hebrew and Yiddish and in this she was aided by her polymath husband.

Several of Rachel's articles were dedicated to Jewish life in the USSR during Stalin's time. "Dashed Hopes", describes the tragic fate of the members of the Jewish Anti-Fascist Committee – Solomon Michoels and Itzik Fefer – and, in particular, their visit to London in 1943. This article is based on the rare booklet "The Russian Jews in the War" published in London in 1943 by the Jewish Fund for Soviet Russia.

Rachel lived in Leningrad during an extraordinary period in the life of Soviet Jews – from 13th January to 5th April 1953 – covering the events of the so called, 'Doctors Plot', ending with the death of Stalin. In one of the articles, she recalls the time when the whole existence of the Jewish community was under threat and only the death of Stalin, which happened on Purim, saved them, giving a new meaning and outlook on the festival of Purim.

Rachel's father joined the Soviet Army when Germany and her allies (including Finland) attacked the USSR in June 1941 and was wounded at the Leningrad front. When he recovered from his injuries, he was appointed the director of a factory where he had worked before the war. This factory replaced their pre-war civilian production with mortars, which went straight from the factory gates to the Front. Rachel's father explained to her that several Jews had been put in charge of the biggest defence plants in Leningrad and other cities and that their efforts played a big part in the victory over the Nazis. Research in this area resulted in one of the chapters in this collection. Another chapter is based on research done in archives in the Finnish capital, Helsinki, where Rachel described a relatively unknown history of Jewish soldiers in the Finnish army, who initially fought with the Germans against the Soviet army.

As mentioned before, Rachel grew up in a city with great art traditions. She was able to attend many exhibitions which took place in Leningrad and other cities in the USSR. She was especially interested in the art by important Jewish painters. When she immigrated to London, she found out that many prominent Jewish painters who worked in the USSR are relatively unknown in Britain. To help bring these Russian Jewish artists to the attention of the public, she published a series of articles about them in *Jewish Renaissance*, included in this collection. One of these is dedicated to Yehuda Pen, the founder of the famous Vitebsk (Belarus) art school, and the teacher of Marc Chagall. One of the best paintings of the young Chagall was on the cover of an issue of the magazine where this article was printed. Rachel describes how she had a chance to see this and other paintings by Yehuda Pen, at that time in storage of the Minsk Art Museum. The reasons why these were put in storage are explained in the article. Two other articles in this collection are dedicated to Soviet-Jewish painters well known in Russia but less than known in the West – Natan Altman and Anatoly Kaplan. Rachel always hoped that one day a special exhibition of the works of Y. Pen, N. Altman, A. Kaplan, and other well-known Soviet-Jewish painters, could be organised in this country. Perhaps one day this dream will become a reality.

Polina Bayvel,
May 2024 (Iyar 5784)

1

Printers and Princes – the Story of Uninterrupted Friendship

Originally published in The Polish Review,
vol. XLV, issue 3, 2000, pp 347-354

This is the story of the uninterrupted friendship between two families: of the Polish Princes Sanguszko and Jewish printers Shapiro from the end of the eighteenth century to the first quarter of the twentieth century! Given the political and social context, it is remarkable how such a friendship could have developed.

Both families lived in Slavuta [in Polish *Slawuta*, and in Yiddish - סלאוויטא], a town in Poland which became Russian after 1793, but is now part of Ukraine. The illustrious family of the Princes Sanguszko owned the whole Volhynia [*Wolynia*] province. This family originated from the clan of Gedymin, a Great Prince of Lithuania, and at the time part of the most powerful states in Europe. Gedymin's descendants were the second most noble aristocracy in the whole of the Russian Empire.

The Shapiros were the descendants of famous rabbis and owned a printing house in Slavuta which produced religious books. It would seem that there could be no chance that these families would establish any close relationship, let alone friendship. But the cruelty of Russian Tsar Nicholas I brought about a strong bond and deep sympathy to common misfortunes. Members of both families were tried in nineteenth century military courts and sentenced to exile in Siberia. Tsar Nicholas personally initiated and supervised both trials. (I heard this story for the first time from my late father, who was born in Slavuta and was one of the descendants of the Shapiro family).

Hieronim Janusz Sanguszko (1743-1812) was the last *wojewoda* (governor) of Volhynia province when Poland was still an independent state [1]. He owned Slavuta, which he made the principal town of Volhynia, building a magnificent palace there, making it his main residence.

Hieronim Janusz was a typical old Polish magnate, unceremonious with the gentry, arrogant with the ordinary people, generally rude, and a lover of horses and hunting. He behaved as a grandee, holding court in his large estate, running up enormous debts despite his ownership of huge ancestral lands. In 1793, after the second partition of Poland, Volhynia was incorporated into Ukraine, then a part of the Russian Empire. Hieronim Janusz kept all his ancestral lands, and the Sanguszko family had great influence until the 1917 Russian October Revolution.

Eustachy (1768-1844) was Hieronim Janusz's only son and heir. From his youth he prepared himself for a military career and went on to study at the French Military Academy in Strasbourg. Afterwards he served in the Polish and French forces and rose to the rank of general. Prince Eustachy took part in the war in 1792 and in the Kosciuszko Uprising of 1794 against Russia. He also joined Napoleon's troops invading Russia, but realising that Napoleon faced defeat, he left the French Army and returned to Slavuta.

The oldest son of Prince Eustachy, Roman Stanislaw (1800-1881) studied at the Berlin University. In 1820, he received an order from Tsar Alexander I to join the Russian Army, where he served in the Guards. Nicholas I was present at his wedding in 1828. In 1830, Prince Roman's wife died giving birth to their daughter and when the Polish November Uprising started, he joined the insurgents. Since he was an officer of the Russian Army, this made him a deserter. When Prince Roman was captured by Russian troops and recognised, he was sentenced to death, but the sentence was later commuted to stripping him of all civil rights, confiscation of all property, and exile to Siberia. Tsar Nicholas, who personally supervised all sentences of Polish noblemen, wrote with his own hand in the margin, 'The authorities are severely warned to take care that this convict walks in chains like any other criminal, every step of the way.'

The chains left scars on Prince Roman's body for the rest of his life and in 1834 his exile was replaced by military service. He was sent to the Caucasus where, as a soldier, he took part in the war against the Chechens. In 1838, he was reinstated to his nobility and officer's ranks. However, it was only in 1845, after a shell shock which left him deaf, that he was allowed to return to Slavuta. Prince Roman did not remarry and lived a very modest and lonely life. He cared not only for his estate but also about improving the life of the people living on the estate, as well as his employees. He became a friend to all the returning exiles, assisting them with money and advice and helping to arrange their affairs and livelihood.

Prince Roman became one of the most famous heroic figures of the Polish aristocracy, glorified for all the sacrifices he made for the freedom of Poland. When writer Joseph Conrad published his short story 'Prince Roman', he became immortalised in world literature.

At this time, the Polish magnates treated the Jews as important to the reconstruction of the cities and the development of foreign trade. In 1791, Moshe Shapiro (1759-1839) became Rabbi of Slavuta [2]. His father was the great and famous Rabbi Pinchas Shapiro from Korets *[Korzec]*, Volhynia. Pinhas Shapiro was a passionate patriot of Poland and hated the rule of Moscow. His descendants remembered a statement which he constantly repeated: "While I am alive, no Russian will set his foot in Volhynia." He died in 1791, before the second partition of Poland [3].

Moshe followed his father's conviction that a man should live by his own toil, and so became an engraver. In 1792, he opened a Jewish printing press in Slavuta with the permission of Hieronim Janusz. The Hebrew letters that he himself engraved were renowned for their beauty and clarity and his skill as an engraver confirmed Moshe as a true artist. In the nineteenth century, for the first time in eastern Europe, Moshe Shapiro printed the entire Babylonian Talmud as well as other religious books. Because of their unusual beauty, clarity of print and excellence of paper and colour, the Slavuta editions enjoyed great fame not only in Russia but also across western Europe. (The Shapiro Talmud was shown at the Jewish printing exhibition at the British Museum in 1995).

Later, Moshe transferred the management of his printing house to his two sons, Shmuel-Abba (Shmuel Avraham Abba) and Pinchas. Under their management it became the largest printing house in the Russian Empire. It was technologically well-organised and had its own typographical plant and paper factory, where Jews and non-Jews were employed in equal numbers. The production of the printing house increased greatly, as did the profits and the Shapiros distributed a large amount to charity. Practically the entire town depended on them for their livelihood, either as workers, employees or sales representatives of the printing house, which meant that the owners had great influence in Slavuta as well as the surrounding region. Thanks to their pedigree and wealth, piety and broad philanthropy, their name was universally renowned and respected.

From the beginning of the reign of Tsar Nicholas I in 1825, the life of Jews in Russia severely deteriorated [4]. Nicholas hated Jewish people because he considered them as eternal arch enemies of Christianity. His aim was to convert all Jews, and during his reign in accordance with his orders the government pursued an unprecedented policy of active intervention in Jewish life. The situation was aggravated because of continuous internal strife. The *mitnagdim* (adherents of rabbinical Judaism) opposed the *hasidim* (adherents of a religio-mystical movement). The *maskilim* (the free-thinking intelligentsia) hated equally both the *mitnagdim* and the *hasidim*. A lot of denunciations came from the Jewish converts to Christianity. The famous historian Saul Ginsburg, who, after the October 1917 Revolution researched the government archives on Jewish life in Russia in the nineteenth century, writes that the informers and their denunciations sent to the government officials were like a plague in Jewish life.

In the 1830s, an especially fierce struggle started in the field of Jewish printing. The *mitnagdim* informed the government that the literature which was disseminated by the *hasidim* was detrimental and dangerous. The denunciations from the *maskilim* reached the various ministries in St. Petersburg regarding the large number of uncensored books published by the *hasidim*. As the Slavuta printing house was the largest and the most prominent in the whole country, the brunt of the attack was directed towards it. On top of this, a bitter strife began between the two main Jewish printing houses, the Slavuta and Vilna [or Wilno, now Vilnius, the capital of Lithuania], competing with each other. The hasidic rabbis supported Slavuta and misnagdic rabbis supported the Vilna printers. The government obtained tendentious and inaccurate information about their dispute from both sides, which resulted in sad consequences for the Jewish printing trade in Russia generally and especially for the Slavuta printers. The soil was febrile and only a spark was needed to provoke a major tragedy.

In 1835, one of the bookbinders employed by the Slavuta printing house was found dead. Apparently, the disgruntled man had taken his own life (he hanged himself in his workplace) because he had recently been fired for drunkenness. The local priest maliciously went to the authorities with the outrageous claim that the Shapiro brothers had actually killed one of their own workers. A Jewish doctor conveniently provided the authorities with a motive for the crime. He supplied the priest with a translation of a page from a Jewish book (he claimed that the book was uncensored) which allegedly stated that the Jews were forbidden to help Christians even when the latter were in mortal danger. The priest claimed that the bookbinder was killed because he intended to deliver this page to the authorities. After the reports of the Slavuta affair arrived in St. Petersburg, Nicholas inscribed in his own hand the following resolution: "All those guilty in this matter should be turned over to the military court and tried with the greatest severity." He showed great interest in the Slavuta case and personally selected Count Vasilchikov as the investigator.

Prince Eustachy Sanguszko held the Shapiros in the highest esteem and greatly trusted and respected them. He knew from his own tragic experience with his son, the cruelty of Nicholas I. Prince Eustachy invited Count Vasilchikov and told him that his family had known the Shapiros for many years and could guarantee their innocence and honesty [5]. However, this did not help as Vasilchikov had an order from the Tsar. The brothers were arrested in 1836 for the alleged murder of the worker who had supposedly denounced them for printing books without permission from the censor. The printing house was closed down.

Later the same priest enlisted help from another Jewish doctor who provided false translations and false testimonies distorting the entire meaning of the book in question. For his services the doctor was generously rewarded with an order issued by the Tsar himself. The money paid to him was taken from the Shapiros' possessions. The Shapiros were sent to Kiev and held in the harshest prison, 'The Fortress'. It was not until 1839, more than three years after the beginning of the trial that the highest military court issued its verdict. Shmuel-Abba and Pinchas were ordered to "run the gauntlet" to be beaten 1500 times, to be deprived of all rights, and sent to Siberia. The verdict of the military court was confirmed by Tsar Nicholas I, who inscribed in his handwriting on the top of the page of the verdict: "so it shall be." The verdict in the Slavuta case had no parallel in the entire history of the Jews of Russia. Old Rabbi Moshe Shapiro, the founder of the Slavuta Printing House, who was to be sent to Siberia, became ill and died of grief in Kiev in 1839.

The Shapiros' punishment was so severe that they were asked for their last request as they were not expected to survive. Pinchas, who was the younger at age 47, was asked to be the first, hoping that this would help Shmuel-Abba, then 55. He also requested to be buried in a Jewish cemetery if he died. The corporal punishment was performed in the following manner: Two rows of soldiers were formed, one opposite the other and with 250 soldiers in each. Each soldier held a wooden rod 1.75 inches thick. The condemned men were stripped to the waist, their hands bound to rifles and two soldiers led them along the two rows as each soldier beat them with his rod. The punishment was usually given in multiples of 500, which meant that the two brothers had to go through the rows three times. In the process of beating Pinchas, one soldier aimed the blow too high, and his skullcap fell off the poor man. Pinchas stopped and refused to go any further until the skullcap was placed back on his head, prolonging his suffering as he received even more blows. This terrible episode inspired famous writers (I. L. Perets and An-ski) to record the incident and a vivid description can be found in their stories. Immediately after this gruesome punishment, the brothers were moved to the military hospital because their wounds were horrendous. It was only at the end of 1839 that they had healed sufficiently for the long journey to Siberia to begin.

The road to Siberia lay through Moscow and the brothers left Kiev bound in chains, proceeding on foot under the guard of a convoy of soldiers, and it was only at the end of 1840 that they arrived in Moscow. There they fell ill and were detained in Moscow Prison until their health improved. At this point information about the subsequent events differs. Encyclopedias (English, German and Russian) say that the Shapiro brothers were sent to Siberia and that the older brother died there. This statement was repeated even in an encyclopedia published in Israel in 1994. This is incorrect and the truth is quite different. From this catastrophe which befell the Shapiro family ultimately something positive transpired. The revulsion about the verdict and the corporal punishment of the brothers was felt by everyone in the Jewish community and proved a catalyst in uniting all the Jews.

The *mitnagim, hasidim, maskilim,* and even some converts to Christianity forgot their disagreements and concentrated their efforts in saving the Slavuta martyrs. Minor officials were bribed and a considerable amount of money was collected to help the brothers survive the harsh prison conditions. Some influential Jews also managed to involve the Governor General of Moscow, Prince Golitsyn, in their fate. The Prince showed a remarkably humane attitude and sent a strongly worded petition to Tsar Nicholas I on behalf of the brothers, asking to allow them to return home because of their poor health. His request was rejected by the Tsar, who presented the following resolution: "If they are ill, they should be left in Moscow in the almshouse." After the Shapiros were given a medical examination, Prince Golitsyn transferred them to the almshouse, so that they were no longer imprisoned nor isolated. They could be visited by their families, have kosher food brought to them regularly and many Jewish merchants visiting Moscow treated them with great respect.

Prince Eustachy, who was already in his 70s, made a special trip to visit the Shapiro brothers and to convey information and greetings from their families. At this time there were no railways in Russia and he had to travel by horse-driven coaches, making the journey hard and tiring. Altogether, they stayed in the almshouse in Moscow for sixteen years. According to the prison rules, a prisoner who was unable to go to Siberia because of bad health had to undergo medical examinations every four months. So, during the sixteen years they underwent 48 medical examinations, each one stating that they were unfit to be sent into exile (in spite of the orders from St. Petersburg!). This could only have happened thanks to the united and endless efforts of the Jews and the humane attitudes of some of the members of the Moscow administration who had the courage to stand up against the wishes of the Tsar.

Count Vasilchikov felt pangs of conscience about the suffering of the Shapiro brothers and in 1848 he tried to obtain their pardon, but Nicholas refused to hear anything about this. After the death of Nicholas in 1855, his son, Alexander II, succeeded him. Count Vasilchikov, who was the Governor General of Ukraine with his main residence in Kiev, sent a petition to the new Tsar. He emphasised that no new evidence had been uncovered during his investigation in 1836 which could be used against the Shapiro brothers, and asked Alexander to allow them to return to Slavuta. In 1856 Tsar Alexander II agreed to Count Vasilchikov's request and the Shapiro brothers were released. The way back from Moscow was triumphal for the Shapiro brothers. Great respect and love was shown to them everywhere. When they arrived in Kiev, Count Vasilchikov invited them to his house and asked their forgiveness for his part in their misfortunes. He explained that he was under specific orders from Nicholas I, which he could not disobey. In Slavuta there was a special celebration. The whole town, from small children to adults, came out to meet them, and everyone wanted to greet the two elders who had come home after twenty years of pain and suffering. One of the brothers became a rabbi in Slavuta and the other in a nearby town. In 1847, their sons re-established a new printing house in a larger city, Zhitomir. Tsar Nicholas I had allowed only two Jewish printing houses to exist in Russia, in Vilna and Zhitomir.

The close friendship between the Princes Sanguszko and the Shapiro family continued long after the death of Shmuel-Abba and Pinchas. The last owner of the Slavuta estate was Prince Roman-Damian Sanguszko (1832-1917). He was a nephew of Prince Roman and studied sciences at the Sorbonne in Paris, and for a period of time was an attaché at the Russian embassy in Berlin. Roman-Damian did not have any children of his own, so he adopted two girls whose mother came from Prince Radziwil's family and died young.

During his life, Slavuta flourished and became one of the most prosperous districts in the whole of Ukraine. It had many factories as well as other enterprises, two banks and even became a resort. Prince Roman-Damian was very benevolent towards the Jewish population of Slavuta (the Jews made up 60 percent of its population). My grandfather worked as a manager at one of Prince Sanguszko's enterprises. All this came to an abrupt end in the autumn of 1917, when a drunken mob of deserters from the Russian Army attacked their magnificent palace. Old Prince Roman-

Damian tried to calm the violent crowd, but it ended tragically for him. He was murdered (although his daughters managed to escape), bringing to the end the life of the Sanguszkos in Slavuta. The attackers looted and destroyed everything which was in their way.

When I visited Slavuta in 1977, the Sanguszko name was still remembered by the local population. I took a photograph of the *kosciol,* the only surviving part of the magnificent palace built by the last *wojewoda,* which the people of Slavuta called "the Sanguszkos' church" My own grandparents were killed by the Nazis in the autumn of 1941, ending the uninterrupted 150-year Shapiro presence in Slavuta. However, the story about the Shapiro brothers has had a postscript. When the brothers eventually left Moscow to return to Slavuta, they took with them a Torah (Scroll of the Law), the history of which is remarkable. Whilst the brothers were in the almshouse, every week the appropriate portion of the Law was specially written and taken to them. Gradually they assembled a full Torah. The Scroll had a symbolic meaning for the Shapiro brothers. It helped to maintain their spirits, gave them hope that they would survive the harshest conditions, and eventually return home as moral victors. The Shapiros' Scroll was kept in the oldest brother's family and always passed to the eldest son. It survived the revolution and civil war in Russia but was confiscated by the Soviet authorities.

After the 1917 revolution, some members of the Shapiro family moved to Poland. One of the descendants of Shmuel-Abba Shapiro, sharing his name, who owned the Brothers Shapiro Scroll before the confiscation, wanted to see it returned. According to a family story, he asked the famous Rabbi Meir Shapiro, who like him was a descendant of Rabbi Pinchas of Korets, for help. Rabbi Meir Shapiro was a member of the Polish Parliament *[Sejm]* during 1922-1927 [6]. Rabbi Shapiro managed to enlist support from Prince Janusz Radziwill (1880-1967), an influential politician, member of the *Sejm,* and a senator, who, from time to time would fulfill important missions entrusted to him by the Polish government. Like the Princes Sanguszko, Prince Radziwil was born in Volhynia and lived there until 1917. In the 1920s, thanks to the mediation of Prince Radziwil, the Shapiro Brothers' Scroll was included in the list of items transferred to Poland in accordance with Article XI of the Riga Peace Treaty. Signed on March 18, 1921, it stipulated the exchange of cultural and religious treasures between Russia, Ukraine and Poland. In this way, the Scroll returned to its rightful owner [7]. Shmuel-Abba Shapiro emigrated from Poland to Palestine with his family in 1937, bringing the Scroll with him. Shmuel-Abba's wife was related to the family of the famous Rabbis Schneerson of the Lubavitch movement. When she died in 1954, Shmuel-Abba decided to present the Scroll to Rabbi M. M. Schneerson, the Rebbe and leader of the Lubavitch movement, living in Brooklyn, New York. Rabbi Schneerson acknowledged this gift in his letter to Shmuel-Abba Shapiro on 1 October 1954, stating [8]: 'I am happy to convey to you the good news that Rabbi B. Gorodetzky brought to me the Sefer Torah (Scroll of the Law) two days before Rosh Hashana [the Jewish New Year] May you be as pleased as I am about this.'

Rabbi Schneerson knew the provenance of the Scroll which made it especially precious. During his life, the Scroll was used on a regular basis in his synagogue in Brooklyn during the most solemn days of the Jewish calendar and is still used there on special occasions.

The fate of the Shapiro Scroll, which outlived the Russian tsars, three revolutions, Lenin, Stalin, persecutions, pogroms, and wars, is the best testament to the words by one of the characters from Mikhail Bulgakov's well known novel *Master and Margarita* which became proverbial: 'Manuscripts do not burn.'

Notes and References

1. Teresa Zielinska, *Poczet Polskich rodow arystokratycznych* [List of Polish Aristocratic Families] (Warsaw: Wydawnictwa Szkolne i Pedagogiczne, 1997).

2. 'Di Slaviter Drama', a series of twelve articles in the *Jewish Daily Forward*, from 12 December 1937 to 27 February, 1938, translated by E. H. Prombaum, *The Drama of Slavuta* by Saul M. Ginsburg (Lanham, New York, and London: University Press of America, Inc., 1991).

3. *Parlament Rzeczypospolitej Polskiej, 1919-1927* [The Parliament of the Polish Republic, 1919-1927] (Warsaw: L. Zlotnicki, 1928), p. 310.

4. M. Stanislawski, *Tsar Nicholas I and the Jews* (Philadelphia: Jewish Publishing Society, 1983).

5. Chava Shapiro, "Achim mi Slavuta [The Brothers from Slavuta], *Hashiloah*, vol.30 (1914), pp. 541-544.

6. Tadeusz and Witold Rzepecki, *Sejm i Senat* [The Sejm and Senate] (Poznan: Wielkopolska KsięgarniaNakladowa Karola Rzepeckiego, 1923), p. 125. He represented the Alliance of Orthodox Jews *[Związek Zydow Ortodoksow]*. His name is given as 'Majer Szapira.'

7. Rabbi Isur Frenkel, *Ichidei segula* [Outstanding Personalities] (Tel-Aviv: Alif Publishers, 1955), pp. 272-276.

8. Rabbi M. M. Schneerson, letter no. 2996, October l, 1954, Iggrot Kodesh, (Brooklyn, New York: Kehot Publication Society, 1989), vol. 10, p. 2.

2

Closed Down by Two Tsars: A short note from a family archive

Originally published in Jewish Culture and History,
vol.5, issue 2, 2002, pp.114-127

This chapter is dedicated to 75 years of the activity of the Shapiro printing houses in Slavuta and Zhitomir and based on the family archives and documents from the Ukrainian and Russian State Archives, which recently became accessible. These documents clearly show the reasons why both the reactionary Tsar Nicholas I and the reformer Alexander II brought their wrath upon several generations of the Shapiro printers, although no laws were violated by the Shapiros, who published their books only with the permission of the censors. The main reason for the closure of the printing houses was because this family of printers followed their religious and ideological principles – which were in contradiction to the official government policy of forcibly 'reforming' the Jewish population.

There are two Russian adages which say that lightning never strikes twice in one place, and bombs never fall twice into the same crater. The story of two Jewish printing houses established by the members of one family and closed down by two Russian Tsars – the first, Nicholas I, the reactionary, called the 'Gendarme of Europe' [1], and the second, his son, Alexander II, a reformer, called the 'Liberator Tsar' – strikingly refute the above adages. The first of the two-family printing houses was established in Slavuta, a small town in Ukraine on the border with Poland. At the end of the eighteenth century, Moshe Shapiro, a son of the famous sage Pinchas of Korets, became its Rabbi and the story of the Slavuta printing house is described in Chapter 1, 'Printers and Princes' [2].

No part of Jewish life escaped the attention of the informers. According to the historian S. M. Ginsburg, Tsar Nicholas I did not believe age-old antisemitic claims that Jews use Christian blood for their rituals; if such a practice existed, Nicholas I explained, then enough informers would be found amongst the Jews to tell the government about it [3]. Opposing factions appealed to the government, accusing their opponents of treason and subversion. Government repression against the Jews was often provoked by these denunciations. To describe this phenomenon Russian Jews used the quotation from Genesis: 'The voice is the voice of Jacob, the hands are the hands of Esau' [4] (Jacob being the symbol of the Jews and Esau, the Russian authorities).

In the 1830s, an especially fierce struggle began in the area of Jewish printing. The mitnagdim informed the government that the literature being disseminated by the hasidim was detrimental and dangerous. The denunciations from the maskilim reached the various ministries in St Petersburg regarding the large number of uncensored books published by the hasidim. As the Slavuta printing house was the largest and the most prominent in the entire country, it bore the brunt of the attack [5].

The printing house was closed down.

Tsar Nicholas I took a personal interest in the Slavuta case and ordered that the brothers be tried by a military court 'with the greatest severity'. The Shapiros were sent to Kiev and held in the harshest prison, the Kiev fortress. It was not until 1839, more than three years after the beginning of the trial, that the highest military court issued its verdict and the punishment, confirmed by Tsar Nicholas I (see Chapter 1).

The old Rabbi Moshe Shapiro, who should have been sent to Siberia, according to the verdict of the military court, died in Kiev in 1839. The brothers survived the corporal punishment and, after recovering in the military hospital, left Kiev bound in chains, proceeding on to Moscow. Thanks to the united and boundless efforts of the Jewish community they were left in Moscow and released in 1856 by Tsar Alexander II. After some 20 years of pain and suffering, the brothers were allowed to return to Slavuta [6].

Following the Shapiros' arrest in 1835 all Jewish printing houses in Russia were closed down by the order of Nicholas I and later he allowed only two Jewish printing houses to be opened in Russia, in Vilna and Zhitomir. In 1847, the sons of the arrested brothers [7] from Slavuta opened a new printing house in Zhitomir, which at the time was the capital of the Volynia province.' The focus of this chapter is on this second Shapiro printing house. Some of the information comes from my family archives. One of the founders of the Zhitomir printing house, Yehoshua Heshel Shapiro, was my great-great-grandfather. Other information comes from the *Collection of documents of the Jewish Historical-Archaeological Commission of the All-Ukrainian Academy of Science* [8, 9], of which only approximately 10 per cent was published in 1928-29; the rest was thought lost and never appeared in academic research publications. It was kept in the secret collection of the Central State Historical Archives of Ukraine and was published, in Russian, only in 1999.[9]

The Zhitomir printing house was a huge and successful enterprise, employing 150 people. The Shapiro brothers printed and distributed books throughout the whole of the South-West Territory (part of the Russian Empire) where there were large concentrations of Jews [10]. Their books were also exported to Western Europe. For the Shapiro family this was not only a business but the continuation of a mission started by their grandfather Moshe. To show that they continued the principles established by their grandfather, they put on the title page of every book published by them, before their names, as owners of the printing house the following line (in Hebrew): 'Grandsons of the Rabbi of Slavuta', i.e. Moshe Shapiro (as shown in Figure 2.1).

The Shapiro family was related to many Hassidic dynasties – Twerski of Chernobyl, Hager of Vizhnits and others. By way of illustration, see the letter, 'To whom it may concern' (Figure 2.2), from Rabbi Aharon, son of the famous Rabbi Mordechai Twerski of Chernobyl. This letter is a preface to the book *Tikunei Hazohar* published by L. and H. Shapiro in Zhitomir in 1865. In this letter Rabbi Aharon informs the public that his 'in-law', 'the famous rich man, Yehoshua Heshel', received permission from the censor to publish the above book. 'The letters in this book,' he says, 'are a pleasure for the eyes'. In view of the high costs incurred in this publication, the publishers and the author of the letter ask competitors to refrain from publishing the book for another ten years.

The significance of this preface can be understood only by reference to the history of the Slavuta printing house [11]. In the early 1800s there were very few of editions of the *Talmud Bavli* [Babylonian Talmud] available because of the numerous burnings of them in previous centuries. The cost of printing was prohibitive as separate plates had to be made for each page. In 1810 the founder of the Slavuta printing house sought the exclusive right to print an entire *Talmud Bavli*. To protect his astronomical financial commitment, he wanted a guarantee from the greatest Jewish scholars of his generation that no other printer would be given permission to print the Talmud. He was granted the exclusive right for 20 years, and between 1817 and 1822 the third printing of the Talmud was published with letters of 'approbation – privilege' from such notable rabbis as Shneur Zalman Schneerson and Levi Itzchak of Berdichev. By 1834 nearly all sets of the Talmud had been sold, and the Shapiros decided to print another edition, as the rabbinical 'approbation' still belonged to them. However, despite this the Romm family in Vilna began preparations to print the *Talmud Bavli*. The Shapiros were angered because they were convinced that they alone had the authority to re print. However, the Vilna printers argued that the exclusive right had been granted to the Shapiro printers only to allow them to sell their books so that they would not lose money. Now that most of the editions had been sold they felt that the Shapiro printers were no longer entitled to retain their exclusive right. Both the Slavuta and Vilna printers went to more than 100 rabbis to petition their case. Each side had prominent scholars who agreed with and defended their respective points of view. The arguments grew into a bitter conflict of accusation (including the accusation of bribery) that enveloped towns and communities throughout Eastern Europe. It is unclear how long this would have continued had the 'Slavuta case' not been brought to an end with the closure of the Shapiro printing house.

Later the mitnagdim supporting the Vilna printers presented the terrible ordeal of the Shapiro family following the 'Slavuta case' as God's punishment for accusing the well-known Rabbi S. Eger of accepting a bribe for the Vilna printers. In 1840 the Romms from Vilna suffered tremendous losses when their printing house was destroyed by a fire. The hasidim, in turn, considered this to be God's punishment for their unfair competition with the Shapiro printing house. In 1865 when Rabbi Aharon Twerski's preface was written, the memory of this conflict was most likely still alive. It is obvious that the aim of the preface was to safeguard the financial interest of his relatives as well as to prevent a repetition of the conflict of 1834-35.

Throughout the existence of the Zhitomir printing house its owners were the object of various denunciations. The first ones [12] were directed by Joseph Sfard, the brother-in-law of Arye-Leib and Lipa Shapiro. Joseph Sfard had business dealings with the Shapiros and from 1849 had some financial claim on them. Apparently, he was unhappy with their offers to settle the claim and in order to extract more money from the Shapiros Joseph Sfard involved a friend asking him to find material compromising the Shapiros with the aim of blackmailing them. The *Jewish Historical Archaeographical Commission* collection of documents contains three letters from this friend to Sfard, which could have come directly from the pages of the great Yiddish writer and humorist Sholem Aleichem [13]. In 1852, when Joseph Sfard's attempt to get more money failed, he sent several denunciations to the local police officer, alleging that the Shapiros had bribed a certain censor and printed two editions of the same book using a single permission. Sfard's denunciation resulted in extensive correspondence between the Kiev Governor-General and the Volynia Governor. The Kiev Governor-General ordered a search of the houses of the printing house owners. Fortunately for the Shapiros, the attempt to compromise them was laughable and could not be upheld. An investigation by the Commission established by the authorities showed that all the accusations were false.

The reign of Tsar Alexander II was the time of the 'Great Reforms'. The authorities undertook some relaxation of anti-Jewish legislation. A steady stream of new laws favourable to select groups of the Jewish population was proclaimed [14]. The merchants of the first (and later of the second and third) guild, craftsmen and those with university degrees were permitted to live anywhere within the Russian Empire. The latter were additionally permitted to enter any branch of state service. As a result of these reforms the number of Jewish students in gymnasia and universities increased greatly. However, the reforms did not eliminate the relative inequality of the Jewish population and resulted in a phenomenon known as 'partial emancipation'. The political principle 'education first and rights afterwards' was in force during this period. In 1865 the Interior Minister, Count A.P. Valuev formulated the aim of government policy towards the Jewish Question: to 'eradicate fanaticism and bring together Jews and the surrounding population' [15]. This policy greatly affected the fate of the Zhitomir printing house.

The success of the Zhitomir printing house attracted the attention of the Russian government because from its point of view the books printed there 'were not useful' and did not help the aims of 'enlightenment' of the Jewish population. This resulted in a supreme decree, issued by the Tsar in 1862, which allowed Jewish printing houses to open without any restrictions – in order to undermine the monopoly of the Shapiros' printing house in the South-West Territory. This decision did not bring the expected results, and, moreover, one of the partners of the Zhitomir printing house, Arye-Leib Shapiro, opened his own printing house which quickly became successful. One of the censors of the Jewish books from the Kiev Censorship Committee presented a memorandum on the Zhitomir printing house to the Kiev Governor-General. The censor discussed the question of the price of the Jewish books based on his visits to the main cities where the Jewish population lived. His conclusion, after a thorough investigation, was that the books published by the Zhitomir printing house were the cheapest in Russia in spite of the very high quality of the print and paper. He added that pious Jews had a special confidence in this printing house because for a very long time it had published only religious books and was considered a spiritual institution. Therefore, their preference was to buy books printed by the Zhitomir printing press [16]. Unfortunately for the Shapiros they fell victims to their own success. In 1864, N. Svarchevsky, an official for special assignments in the office of the Volynia Governor, sent a report to the Governor on the harmful influence of Shapiros' printing house. He wrote: "The Zhitomir printing house was opened in 1847, as the only institution in the South-West Territory, and had to assist through their publications in the enlightenment of the Jewish population. The Shapiros clearly did not understand their role in achieving these aims. They had strong hasidic beliefs, and, therefore, instead of printing useful books, they printed only religious books in huge quantities. Thus they exerted very harmful influence on the mental and moral development of the Jewish population. Hasidism, the terrible plague of our Jewry, found for itself the right tool - this printing house, and the tzaddikim, the leaders of the hasidim, glorified the Shapiros' enterprise and by ascribing a special sanctity to their publications, helped to increase their sales. The supreme decree issued in 1862 by Tsar Alexander II, allowing the Jewish printing houses to open without restrictions, had not had any effect, because the new competitors did not enjoy the support of the tzaddikim, as in the case of the Shapiros. The harm of the Shapiros' activities is significantly more dangerous than the harm of the tzaddikim, because the latter operate in isolated areas. However, since the Shapiro family is related to many tzaddikim and has strong hasidic beliefs, there is no hope that they can change the direction of their printing house to the better. Therefore, this harmful enterprise deserves immediate closure" [17].

The Censor of Jewish Books, an old maskil, Kh. Z. Slonimsky, sent a list of books to A.P. Bezak, the recently appointed Kiev Governor-General, by the Zhitomir printing house published between 1852 and 1866 [18]. From this list it could be seen that of the 486 printed books during these 15 years all were religious – not one was secular [19]. This fact made an enormous impression on A.P. Bezak, who was very anti-hasidic. He immediately sent a long letter to the Interior Minister, Count P.A. Valuev, including in his letter all the conclusions drawn by N. Svarchevsky. In particular, he insisted that 'the power of tzaddikim in the South West Territory has no limits and is harmful, not only to the Jews but also to the general security" [20]. He considered the closure of the Shapiros' printing house an urgent necessity. In spite of understanding that this action contradicted existing legislation, since the Shapiros published only books that were approved by the censors, he pointed out that it would be necessary to take appropriate steps to 'eliminate this evil'. Bezak asked Count Valuev to seek the Tsar's assent to close the Shapiros' printing house.

Taking into account that under the existing legislation it was impossible to close the Shapiros' printing house by a court decision, Valuev submitted on 18 April 1867 a special petition to the Cabinet of Ministers. The Cabinet fully agreed with his proposals, and on 29 April 1867 Tsar Alexander II approved the Special Decree of the Cabinet of Ministers regarding the closure of the Shapiros' printing house. This was the end of 75 years of the Shapiro family's activities in Jewish printing, achieved only by bending the laws of the Russian Empire.

This was a terrible blow for the owners of the printing house. From their point of view, they had not broken any of the existing laws and regulations. They and their employees were left without means to support themselves. They still had some hope that the authorities' decision could be reversed or another solution could be found. Lipa and Heshel Shapiro submitted an application to the Governor-General asking him to allow the printing house to remain open for another five years to enable the completion of books which had already been begun, to complete the editions of the Talmud and to settle financial accounts. With reference to Shapiros' application, Governor-General A.P. Bezak sent a letter to the Volynia Governor in which he informed the latter that he refused to comply with the Shapiros' request. Moreover, he pointed out that it was the Governor's duty to ensure that none of the Shapiros continued their printing activities or arranged such activities to be continued through third parties or under another name.

Even after receiving such a refusal, the Shapiros continued their attempts to save the printing house. They found a certain Isaac Bakst, a teacher in the Zhitomir Rabbinic Seminary, who was familiar with the printing business and who agreed to serve as a front man. He was a credible candidate because this seminary was one of the main institutions supported by the Russian state with the goal of enlightening the Jews of the Empire. Lipa and Heshel Shapiro sent another application to the Kiev Governor-General asking his permission to let the printing house to Isaac Bakst. Upon receiving this application, the Kiev Governor-General ordered the Volynia Governor to investigate whether the Bakst printing house had, in fact, belonged to the Shapiros. The Volynia Governor later reported to the Governor-General that, as was suspected, Bakst was only the front man, and thus, his printing house should be closed.

In 1869 a new Governor-General of the South-West Territory was appointed, following the death of his predecessor. The Shapiro family decided to take this opportunity to try to reverse the decision to close down their printing house, and that very year Lipa Shapiro's wife, Sura Ita sent a letter to the new Governor-General, Prince A.M. Dondukov-Korsakov. This application is a remarkable document and its translation from the original Russian is reproduced here in full. In this letter, one can see that in spite of all the liberal reforms the Russian Jews were still deprived of elementary rights and had to suffer humiliation. At the same time the letter demonstrates a sophisticated understanding of the mentality of Russian officialdom – the attempts by the author to flatter the *nachalnik* [high official] and to ingratiate herself to him.

The Application

Your Excellency,
   Considering as a good omen for myself and for our suffering family, the comforting passing of Your Excellency through our district, I take the liberty to present to you a most humble request. A supreme decree on the closure of my husband's printing house in Zhitomir became valid in June 1867 on the submission of Your Excellency's predecessor. This unexpected blow struck all of us: myself, my husband and 150 families, dependent on this printing house for their livelihood, like thunder. It plunged us into despair, leaving us speechless. Our printing house was established in 1847 and for over 20 years we conducted business with impeccable honesty, printing only the books approved by censors, and published without any restrictions by all other Jewish printing houses. We never gave any reasons which may have led to the displeasure of the authorities. However, ill-meaning competitors undermined the authorities' trust in us through false denunciations. We were defamed before the Governor-General and the Interior Minister, and – what is most regrettable, the Holy Face of His Imperial Majesty. My husband's and his partner's activities in the printing house were presented as wrong and sinister. They were accused of being the enemies of the general security of the Russian State. There were also denunciations that they refused to publish useful, modern books, and instead they only published and disseminated the kabbalistic and hasidic books as well as the writings of the contemporary tzadikkim and by doing this exerted a harmful influence on the mental and moral state of the Jewish people. If all these facts were

truthful, our guilt would be indeed enormous and unforgivable, and the closure of the printing house would be too lenient a punishment. But because we have a clear conscience, we completely reject all these denunciations and consider them as slander. During the last 20 years of the existence of our printing house not a single book, not a single page was published without prior approval by the censors. We are commercial people, and we are not interested in the contents of the books and publish only the books approved by the censors, who have signified by their signature that the books are conducive to the common good. It is not us who should be accused, but the censors who contravened the existing regulations. In the meantime the authorities, based only on the denunciations of the evil slanderers, carried out this order without giving us the opportunity to present our case. The rapid implementation of this decision did not give us time to settle our numerous commercial dealings, the total value of which comes to 150,000 silver roubles. Our credit was undermined and we have been brought to the brink of shameful bankruptcy. We and one hundred and fifty families who earned their living exclusively by their work in the printing house have been plunged into poverty and disaster.

Your Excellency, the law which punishes the criminal and acquits the innocent is equal for all the loyal subjects of Russia. Why are we deprived of the protection of the courts where mercy and truth triumph? A man accused of murder has the right to defence. Why are we – who have a clear conscience - deprived of this mercy?

Your Excellency, in our application we do not ask for mercy, but the right of access to a court which is merciful and impartial. Let a rigorous investigation based on the laws decide our case and prove our guilt. We will obediently accept a just sentence of the impartial court. We are totally confident that after an official investigation our innocence will be revealed and it will be proved that the closure of our printing house was only the result of the slanders of our competitors. We set all our hopes on the magnanimity and protection of Your Excellency as a great protector and representative of the public interests. Please, Your Excellency, considering our dire situation, present our case to His Imperial Majesty. We hope that taking into account our innocence, he will allow us to re-open our printing house. The local authorities and the representatives of all estates and faiths residing in the Volynia province who know us will vouch for our integrity and loyalty. We and many other families will eternally pray for you as our angel-saviour whose good deeds will save us from inevitable ruin.

I hope to receive a positive answer from Your Excellency, Sura Ita Shapiro [21]

This application by S-I Shapiro was submitted on 12 May 1869. She did not have to wait long for her answer. By 31 May 1869 a reply from the Governor-General to the local district police officer in a letter advised the latter to announce to the applicant that her request to reopen the printing house would not be granted. Clearly, the decision had been made at the provincial rather than the ministerial level.

The last attempt by the Shapiro family to reverse this decision was an application sent to Prince A.M. Dondukov-Korsakov by another member of the Shapiro family. In this application, Moshe Shapiro, the son of I-H Shapiro, wrote the following:

I am totally convinced of the innocence of my parents but even if their guilt could be proved, they have already been punished by being deprived for a long time of the means to earn a living. In any case if permission to re-open the printing house could not be granted to my parents, please do not refuse me, the innocent son, to open the printing house set up by my ancestors, where only books approved by the censors will be published. [22]

Again a refusal followed within two weeks. The closure of the Zhitomir printing house in 1867 was an important event in the history of the Russian government's Jewish policies during this period and made a very distressing impression on the Jewish population of Volynia and Podolia [23]. It proved once more that, despite the radical political changes within Russia, the authorities were continuing to follow the old policy of enforced 'reforming' of the Jews, aimed towards their total assimilation. At the same time the sad history surrounding the closure of the Shapiro printing house was evidence that the outdated views prevailing in the first 30 years of the nineteenth century on the danger of Hasidism and the need for an unrelenting struggle with it, were very much alive some 30-40 years later, in contradiction to the official principle of tolerance. However, the closure was one of the last cases of the influence of those views on practical policy in the 'Jewish Question' during the reign of Alexander II. With the closure of the Zhitomir printing house, one of the main factors irritating the authorities in relation to Jewish printing finally disappeared, through the arbitrariness of supreme power. As in 1836 when all the Jewish printing houses were closed by the decree of Tsar Nicholas I because of the activities of the Shapiros in Slavuta, the Zhitomir printing house was now closed by the decree of Alexander II, contradicting the existing laws and regulations in order to end the activities of printers strictly adhering to their religious and ideological principles [24].

Notes and References

1. Michael Stanislawski, *Tsar Nicholas I and the Jews* (Philadelphia: Jewish Publishing Society, 1983)
2. Rachel Bayvel, 'Printers and princes', *The Polish Review*, 45.3 (2000), 347-54 and Chapter 1 in this volume.
3. Saul M. Ginsburg, *Historical Works* [Yiddish] (New York: S.M. Ginsburg Testimonial Committee, American Jewish Historical Society, 1937), I.
4. *Genesis*, 27:22.
5. *The Drama of Slavuta by Saul Moiseyevich Ginsburg* (Langam, New York and London: University Press of America, 1991).
6. Chava Shapiro, 'Achim mi Slavuta', *Hashiloah*, 30 (1914), 541-4; Isur Frenkel, *Ichidei segula* [Hebrew] (Tel Aviv: Alif Publishers, 1955), pp.272-6.
7. Arie-Leib and Chanina-Lipa, also known as Leiba and Lipa in official documents, were sons of Shmuel-Abba Shapiro, and Yehoshua-Heshel, also called Heshel or Hessel in official documents, was a son of Pinchas Shapiro.
8. *Collection of documents of the Jewish Historical-Archaeographical Commission of the All Ukrainian Academy of Science*, vol. I ed. by Galam (Kiev: 1928); vol. II ed. by Acad A.E. Krymsky (Kiev, 1929).
9. *Collection of documents of the Jewish Historical-Archaeographical Commission of the All Ukrainian Academy of Science*, compiled by Victoria Khiterer (Kiev: Institute of Judaics, 1999).
10. The South-West Territory consisted of three Ukrainian provinces [gubernias], namely, Kiev, Volynia and Podolia.
11. *Dmitry A. Elyashevich, Government Policy and Jewish Printing in Russia* [Russian] (St Petersburg: Mosty Kultury, 1999), p.603.
12. *Jewish Historical-Archaeographical Commission* (see note 9), p.97 (doc. 2.20), p.98 (doc. 2.21, 2.22), p.99 (doc. 2.23).
13. 13. Ibid., p.99 (doc. 2.24), p.100 (2.25, 2.26).
14. John D. Klier, *Imperial Russia's Jewish Question* (Cambridge: Cambridge University Press, 1995), pp.13-31.
15. Elyashevich (see note 11), pp.269-71.

16. *Jewish Historical-Archaeographical Commission* (see note 9), pp.91-2 (doc. 2.15).
17. Ibid, pp.93-95 (doc 2.16, 2.17).
18. Elyashevich (see note 11), pp.273-5.
19. These figures show that the Zhitomir printing house, which published more than 30 books per year, was at that time one of the largest in the Russian Empire (together with the firm of the widow and brothers Romm in Vilna). See Elyashevich (note 11), p.636.
20. Elyashevich (see note 11), pp.273-5.
21. *Jewish Historical-Archaeographical Commission* (see note 9), pp.105-7 (doc. 2.32).
22. Ibid., pp.107-8 (doc. 2.34).
23. Elyashevich (see note 11), p.637, 272.
24. Ibid., p. 237, 272.

3

Who was Rabbi Natan Spira

Originally published in The Polish Review,
vol. L, issue 2, 2005, pp 187-191

In June 2002 a picture of Prince Charles – now King Charles III – visiting the oldest Jewish cemetery in Krakow appeared in many British newspapers. The picture was taken when Prince Charles paid tribute to the great sage Rabbi Natan Nota ben Szlomo Spira (Szpira, Shapiro) (1585-1633). Not many people know who Rabbi Natan Spira was and why he was so honored 370 years after his death.

Besht [1], the founder of Hassidism, once said that the Shapiro family is one of the three families, most ancient and distinguished in their ancestry [2]. The family originated from the town of Speyer in the Rhineland, Germany, from which comes its surname (in different countries and in different periods of time the family name was Spiro, Spira, Szpira, Schapiro, Shapiro). The Jewish community of Speyer was one of the first in the Rhineland to suffer during the First Crusade (on May 3, 1096). After this event, one member of the family, Szimszon (Samson) Spira, left Speyer. He was the first of the family to reach Poland and later served as a Rabbi in Poznan [3]. One of the descendants of Rabbi Szimszon Spira (and ancestor of Rabbi Natan Spira) was Szlomo (Salomon) Spira (1380-1451) who was the Chief Rabbi of Heilbron and Landau in Germany [4]. Szlomo Spira's own grandfather was Treves Mattathias of Provence (1325-1385) who was appointed by King Charles V as the Chief Rabbi of Paris. He founded a *yeshiva* (rabbinical college) which had a large number of students (it was extremely important because of the acute shortage of learned rabbis at that time).

Rabbi Natan Spira was a grandson of the famous Rabbi of Grodno after whom he was named. His father, Szlomo Spira, was a Rabbi in Krakow where Natan was born in 1585. At a young age Natan had shown exceptional abilities. He studied not only the Talmud and Kabbalah, but also philosophy, astronomy and mathematics. He possessed an extraordinary mathematical mind, and where most people think in words he thought in numbers. Rabbi Spira was a prominent Kabbalist, philosopher and a man of great erudition who knew the whole rabbinical literature by heart [5]. A rich Jew, Moses Jakubowicz, chose Natan as a husband for his daughter Rosa, and from that time Natan became free of concerns about earning a living and could immerse himself entirely in his studies.

Rabbi Spira lived in Kazimierz. This was a separate Jewish town on the outskirts of Krakow, then Poland's capital and the city where Jews, who resided in Kazimierz, earned their living. In 1617, Rabbi Natan Spira became rector of the Krakow *yeshiva* where he taught students the Talmud with commentaries, and since then exerted direct influence on young and old people alike [6]. He was considered the best *darshan* [preacher] and a holy man by his contemporaries. During the last years of his life he served also as head of the Rabbinical Court. Interestingly, Rabbi Spira did not take a salary from the community, he gave a lot of money to poor people and donated many valuable items to his synagogue. People from the whole of Poland came to him to solve their problems connected with observing religious rules and regulations [7].

Rabbi Natan Spira was a proponent of practical Kabbalah and introduced it to Polish Jewry. He wrote two Kabbalistic commentaries to the Bible under the title *Megalleh Amukkot* [Discovering Concealed Mysteries] which became classic books of practical Kabbalah. Both books were published after his death, one by his son in Krakow in four volumes in 1636-1639; the other in Lwòw in 1795. The books were reprinted many times and are still widely read by the followers of Kabbalah. Rabbi Spira's contemporaries believed that due to his knowledge of Kabbalah, he possessed a special power; that every night, the prophet Elijah came to him, that Elijah and he bemoaned the despondency of Jewish people and together with the angels in heaven they prayed for the deliverance of Israel. His son wrote in the foreword to *Megalleh Amukkot* that the prophet Elijah appeared when his father was praying in the middle of the night.

To understand why Rabbi Natan Spira was considered one of the greatest men of his time, and was so revered by his contemporaries, it is necessary to know the historical background which determined the life of the Polish Jewry in the sixteenth and seventeenth centuries.

The sixteenth century was the "Golden Age" of the Polish Jewry, a time of absence of intolerance and persecution, during which the Jewish spiritual life flourished. In the last years of the sixteenth century the situation of Polish Jewry changed dramatically for the worse. The wars with Russia, Sweden and Turkey substantially decreased the Jewish population of Poland but the greatest danger was the rebellions of peasants and Cossacks who hated the Jews whom they considered their main oppressors. The extermination of Jews was one of the aims of Cossack rebellions and terrible pogroms occurred during the life of Rabbi Natan Spira.

In the process of the Counter-Reformation some Catholic clergy actively resorted to anti-Jewish actions. In 1631, a Jew from Przemysl was accused of blood libel and was sentenced to death. When this news reached Krakow, Catholics started to see if any Christian child was lost from among them. As it happened, a child had indeed disappeared. A Jewish scholar, Asher Anselm (he was a descendant of Doctor Samuel, personal physician to Queen Bona) was arrested on the suspicion that he murdered the child. The local court condemned him to death. In 1631, Asher Anselm was burned alive. He was praying until the last moment of his life, and like all Jewish martyrs, died with the words "Shema Israel" ("Hear, O Israel") on his lips. Rabbi Natan Spira wrote a special prayer in Anselm's memory which was recited in all Krakow synagogues for several centuries [8].

Natan Spira was well informed about the worsening situation of the Polish Jewry due to external and internal circumstances. He had a foreboding of an imminent major catastrophe awaiting the Jewish people and tried to find ways to avert it. Future events showed that he was right. The catastrophe occurred in 1648-54 when the Cossacks and peasants under the leadership of Bohdan Chmielnicki (Khmelnitsky) exterminated two thirds of the Jewish population of Ukraine. One of the victims was Rabbi Spira's son Shlomo (1616-1650). An exceptionally gifted child, Shlomo gave lessons on Kabbalah when he was seven years old, and later became a Rabbi in the town of Satanow where he was murdered.

In the first quarter of the 17th century the Jewish population of Poland became desperate. Its situation was exacerbated by the fact that many were descendants of immigrants from all the troubled parts of Europe (Germany, Italy, Bohemia, Spain, and Portugal) who found shelter in Poland and had nowhere to run. Every day news came to Krakow about pogroms in different Jewish communities. In these difficult times of hopelessness, Jewish community leaders could only wring their hands and, with grief, look towards an uncertain future.

The Jews of Poland turned to their spiritual leader Rabbi Natan Spira for moral support, comfort and hope for a better future. His Kabbalistic teaching stated that the scattering of Jewish people among other nations and transmigration of souls are a punishment for their sins. He believed that a person's actions in this world affected the higher world as well, and thus his/her fate. The main aim of Rabbi Spira's teaching was the separation of good and evil and bringing forward the salvation of Jews. According to his beliefs, all Jews by virtue of their good deeds can speed up the deliverance of Israel and the whole of mankind. Rabbi Spira's sermons, which made a strong impression on audiences, inspired courage and hope that the Messiah would come and save his people. Many times in the evenings, when Jews who were returning from Krakow to Kazimierz passed the impressive Basilica of the Virgin Mary (Kosciol Mariacki), they looked towards its bell tower and wondered if the prophet Elijah was staying there in readiness to call true believers to go with him to the Holy Land [9].

After Rabbi Natan Spira's premature death his grateful pupils put a memorial stone on his grave with the following inscription: "Here is buried G-d's holy man, who discovered concealed mysteries and saw the prophet Elijah face to face, a genius, head of the Rabbinical Court, head of a *yeshiva,* Natan Nota Spira." The grave of Rabbi Natan Spira became, and still is, a place for pilgrimage. Near the tombstone special boxes were installed to enable visitors to insert notes with requests for help.

Prince Charles spent nearly thirty minutes touring the Kazimierz cemetery, which is 500 years old, and spent a few moments alone in reflection. During the Second World War, residents covered the cemetery to hide its headstones from the Germans. The Prince said: "Thank goodness they didn't destroy it."[10] King Charles is currently at the head of a World Jewish Relief project to build a Jewish community centre in Krakow. This project is particularly timely because in 2005 the 700th anniversary of the Jews settling in Krakow will be commemorated. Everyone who visits Krakow now can see and understand the great achievements of the Polish Jewish community and also the Jewish religious and philosophical legacy, which has not been erased, even by the tragedy of the Holocaust.

Notes and References

1. Israel Ben Eliezer (c. 1700-1760). Also known as Baal Shem Tov (Master of the Good Name) or Besht. Founder of Hassidism.
2. Meir Wunder, Elef Margaliot [Thousand Pearls] (Jerusalem: Institute of the History of the Jews of Galicia, 1993), p. 77.
3. Meir Wunder, p. 219. See also *Parlament Rzeczypospolitej Polskiej,1919-1927* (The Parliament of the Polish Republic, 1919-1927) (Warsaw: L.Zlotnicki, 1928), p. 310.
4. Arye Maimon and Yacov Guggenheim, eds. *Germania Judaica* (Tuebingen: Ortschaftartikel Aach-Lyche, I.C.B.Mohr, 1987).

2

5. Zofia Borzyminska and Rafal Zebrowski, eds. *Polski slownik judaistyczny* [Polish Judaic Dictionary] (Warsaw: Proszynski, 2003), vol. 2, p. 567.
6. Majer Balaban, *Historja Zydów w Krakowie i na Kazimierzu* [History of Jews in Krakow and Kazimierz] (Krakow: Nadzieja, 1931).
7. Meir Wunder, pp. 211-217.
8. Balaban, vol. 1, p.180.
9. Balaban, vol. 2, p. 41.
10. The London Times, 14 June 2002.

4

Life and Activities of Rabbi Meir Shapiro: New Information Based on Documents from the Polish Archives

Originally published in Scripta Judaica Cracovensia,
Krakow, Poland, vol. 5, 2007, pp 7-12

This chapter is dedicated to Rabbi Meir Shapiro, one of the important Jewish personalities of the twentieth century whose ideas were the restoration of the *Yeshivah Chachmei Lublin* and the *Daf Yomi* (page-a-day) Talmud study programme. He was a member of the Polish Parliament (Sejm) and many valuable documents related to his life and activities are kept in Polish archives (especially in the Archive of the Polish Parliament) which have recently become accessible. This chapter is based on these documents.

In 1923 at the first World Congress of Agudat Israel in Vienna the legendary Rabbi Meir Shapiro of Poland proposed the *Daf Yomi* Talmud study programme. The study of one page a day for 2702 days would enable the Torah scholar and layman alike to achieve the completion of the whole of *Shas* (the Babylonian Talmud). It has since grown into a worldwide movement in every major Jewish community. On the 2 February 1931 the first *Siyum* (conclusion) of the study of Talmud according to the *Daf Yomi* programme was celebrated. Hundreds of thousands of people all over the world participated in the celebration of the 11th *Siyum* on 1 March 2005. This event attracted a great interest to the life and activities of Rabbi Meir Shapiro whose brainchild was the *Daf Yomi*.

During 1922–1927 Rabbi Meir Shapiro was a member of Sejm (Polish Parliament). Because of this position many documents related to his biography are preserved in several Polish archives, especially in the Archive of the Sejm. This article is based on these documents.

In the materials kept in the Polish archives, the name Meir Shapiro is given as Majer Szapira or Jehuda Majer Szapira. Among these documents there are two books [1,2] with the biographies of all members of the Sejm from 1919 to 1927. The book *Parlament* [1] specifically lists some information about Meir Shapiro's ancestry. It is most likely that this information came from Rabbi Shapiro himself but it really needs to be analysed and compared with the information from other sources.

Rabbi Meir Shapiro's ancestors, both from his father's and mother's side, were well-known rabbis who had played a prominent part in the life of Jewish community of Poland. One of the ancestors of Rabbi Shapiro, as a child, survived the massacre of the Jews by the Crusaders in 1096 and later came to Poland. He took the surname Spira derived from his birthplace Speyer, a town in the Rhineland, Germany. In Poland, the family Spira-Szapira produced many outstanding personalities, over several generations, some of whom were rabbis in Cracow, then the capital of Poland. It is safe to assume that the authors of *Parlament* had in mind the famous rabbinic names which are known from other sources, namely Natan Spira of Grodno [3] and his grandson Natan Spira of Crakow [4]. Rabbi Natan Spira (1585–1633) was born in Cracow (as already described in Chapter 3) where his father Solomon (Shlomo) served as a rabbi. He was the Rector of the Cracow Yeshivah and the Head of the Rabbinical Court. Rabbi Natan Spira was a famous Kabbalist and wrote a book *Megalleh Amukkot,* reprinted many times and still used by the followers of Kabbalah. Among the ancestors of Meir Shapiro there is a name of one of the most famous rabbis of his generation, the Hasidic Rabbi Pinchas Shapiro of Korets [5]. He was a passionate patriot of Poland and hated Moscow. Descendants of Rabbi Pinchas kept in their memory a statement which he often repeated: "While I am alive, no Muscovite will set his foot on the land of Volhynia" [6]. He did not live to see the two last partitions of Poland and died in September 1791. It is also necessary to mention that the book *Parlament* is the only source where the above statement by Rabbi Pinchas of Korets is cited, despite extensive literature concerning his life and work.

It should be mentioned that there are doubts concerning the statement made in Meir Shapiro's biography in *Parlament* about the child escaping the massacre in Speyer. Professor Yacov Guggenheim is of an opinion that the story of the child's escape in 1096 from Speyer to Poland "is a pious uninformed family legend" [7]. According to Meir Wunder, the first member of the Spira family was Szimszon (Samson) Spira who left Speyer in 1096 after the crusaders' attack on Jews and reached Poland where he served as a rabbi in Poznan.

The database *Deputies and Senators of the Second Polish Republic 1919–1939* [8] and other documents kept in the Archive of the Sejm and the

Archive of New Documents (Warsaw) contain detailed information related to the life and activities of Rabbi Meir Shapiro. Meir Shapiro was born in 1887 in a small town in Bukovina, then a part of Austro- Hungarian Empire. This town is called Suczawa in all Polish documents (it is in Romania now and is called Suceava). His parents were Jacob Samson and Margula (née Schorr). Meir took his first lessons in Jewish and secular subjects in Suczawa. He showed outstanding abilities very early in life and when only nine years of age wrote an extensive work on Judaic theology. At twelve Meir went to study Talmud with his grandfather, a rabbi in Monasterzyska. At fourteen he gave a public lecture in Suczawa synagogue and at sixteen wrote a theological work on astronomy based on his study on the Talmud. At the age of 23 he published this work under the title *Imrej Daat* [2] . Meir Shapiro was ordained as a rabbi by the famous rabbis of his days.

After his marriage in 1907 Rabbi Shapiro lived in Tarnopol where he began social activities in the field of education. He established wide-ranging religious, cultural and political ties, including the Jewish society *Tiferes Hadas* which he supported till the end of his life. This society was an important factor in social life in Tarnopol. Local work prepared Rabbi Shapiro for activities in an incomparable more broad field. In 1910 he started his professional career as a rabbi in a small town Gliniany near Lvov. One of his main interests was religious education of young people. He was a founder of the Yeshivah *Bnei Tora* for which he built a spacious building in Gliniany. In 1912 he participated on the Constituent Assembly of Agudat Israel World organization in Katowice. As its co-founder, Rabbi Shapiro became one of the most important leaders of Agudat Israel which started its active work after First World War. In 1919 he was elected a chairman of the Education Committee of Agudat Israel (Poland) and in 1921 Rabbi Shapiro was invited to became a rabbi in Sanok. In 1922 at the second Polish conference of Agudat Israel, Rabbi Shapiro was elected a chairman of the Executive Committee.

In 1922 Rabbi Meir Shapiro was also elected as a member of Sejm on the list N16 (Bloc of national minorities of the Polish Republic) from the constituency N1 (Warsaw). According to the Sejm he was a member of the Club of the Orthodox Union "Shlomei Emunei Israel" which was a part of a greater Jewish group. Rabbi Shapiro did not show excessive activity as a member of the Parliament. He never spoke during the sessions or was a member of any of the parliamentary committees. During his term as a member of Parliament he only once introduced a parliamentary interpellation on 5 June 1923 on a case of a "railway official forbidding the

Jewish passengers to pray in the carriages if they put on their holy phylacteries" [8]. During his time as a member of Parliament Rabbi Shapiro became a Jewish spokesman in Polish government circles. Dr Wojciech Kulisiewicz justifies the low level of Rabbi Shapiro's activity as a member of Sejm by his many duties as a Rabbi and one of the leaders of Agudat Israel [9]. As already mentioned, the World Congress of the Agudat Israel in Vienna in 1923 elected Rabbi Shapiro to become a member of its Executive Committee. At this Congress he put forward two great ideas which were met with universal approval, the first being the restoration of the great Talmudic Academy in Lublin, and the second the project of *Daf Yomi*. The implementation of these ideas immortalised his name and Rabbi Shapiro carried out these projects from 1923 until his death in 1933.

It is interesting to see how his activities are described in the documents kept in the Polish archives. In 1924 Meir Shapiro became a Rabbi in Piotrkow, so it is surprising that he found enough time for scholarly work in his profession. The result of many years work was an extensive monograph under the title *Or Hameir* which was published in 1926. The Rabbinical conference in Warsaw in 1926 elected Rabbi Shapiro as a member of the Presidium of the Union of Polish rabbis. In Piotrkow, Meir Shapiro published his own weekly political journal *Unser Leben* over a long period of time He also wrote articles in the Warsaw orthodox newspaper *Der Jud*.

Many encyclopaedias, books and articles [10–13] give the date and the place of the death of Meir Shapiro as 1934, Lodz. According to Dr Wojciech Kulisiewicz, the Director of the Library of Polish Parliament, the date of the death of Rabbi Meir Shapiro is registered in the edition XV N 355/1933 of the Lublin Registry Office. The entry made on 27 October 1933 states that Jehuda Majer Szapiro, the son of Jacub Samson and Margula died on this day. According to Dr Wojciech Kulisiewicz, the official who entered the above data made a mistake, spelling the name of the deceased as Szapiro instead of Szapira. Dr Kulisiewicz [14] wrote in his letter to the author that considering this evidence all data of the death relating to Rabbi Shapiro which differ from the ones indicated in the Lublin Registry book should be considered as erroneous.

According to the Jewish calendar, Meir Shapiro died on the 7 of *Cheshvan* 5694. The Jewish year 5694 corresponds to 1933/34, but only several months of the year 5694 fall in 1933, and *Cheshvan* is one of them. Prof. Jonathan Webber [15] pointed out that errors of this kind occur very often when events, the dates of which are established according to the Jewish calendar, occur in the first months of the Jewish year (from *Tishri to Kislev*) and the last months of the civic year (September– December).

As mentioned, Rabbi Shapiro put forward the idea of restoring the great Talmudic Academy in Lublin. His idea was to establish a centre of learning that would become famous not only in Poland but also throughout the world. The first Talmudic Academy in Lublin was created in 1567 and became a world leader in Talmudic studies. Among the teachers in the Yeshivah were internationally renowned scholars whose fame reached far beyond Poland. This Academy functioned until the second half of the seventeenth century. The documents in the Sejm database [8] contain detailed information about the mammoth work undertaken by Rabbi Meir Shapiro in order to implement his idea. The foundation stone for the Yeshivah was laid on 22 May 1924 and Rabbi Shapiro proposed to give the restored institution its former name – the *Yeshiva Chachmei Lublin* (the Academy of the Scholars of Lublin). In order to collect the necessary funds (1 million zlotych) Rabbi Shapiro visited Austria, Czechoslovakia, France, Germany, Belgium,Holland, England and also spent a year in USA. In Polish archives there are excerpts from newspapers published in Poland and the countries visited by Meir Shapiro reporting about various meetings organised by local Jewish groups in support of his campaign.

In the 26 July 1924 issue the Warsaw weekly newspaper *Der Jud* (The Jew) reported: 'The Piotrikow rabbi and member of Sejm Meir Shapiro, while on his way to London, stopped in Vienna to discuss with the members of Central Committee of Agudat Israel the campaign *Keren Hatorah* (Foundation of Torah) which was undertaken in order to collect money for the construction of the Yeshivah in Lublin' [16].

After Vienna, Rabbi Shapiro visited Bratislava (then in Czechoslovakia, now the capital of Slovakia) and Prague. 30 July 1924 the Strasbourg newspaper *Les Dernieres Nouvelles* [13] reported that a public meeting with the participation of Rabbi Shapiro was organised 28 July 1924 by the group "Friends of Jewish Tradition" in a hall of the *Palais des Fetes*. The meeting was attended by the Polish consul in Strasbourg Jan Derezinski. The consul was so impressed by the eloquent and inspiring address of Rabbi Meir Shapiro that he sent off a correspondent's report about the speech to the Polish telegraphic news agency, and the report appeared in all the Polish newspapers. The topic of Rabbi Shapiro's speech was "The moral state of Judaism in Poland." Rabbi Meir Shapiro mentioned his efforts of restoring the Yeshivah in Lublin and asked local Jews to support his project. The Strasbourg newspaper *La Tribune Juive* in its issue of 1 August 1924 published an article by Meir Shapiro, titled *Pressburg – Prague– Strasbourg* [13]. The author of that article is referred to as "The Senior Rabbi and the member of the Sejm." In this article Rabbi Shapiro described his impressions of the Jewish communities he just visited (the author called Bratislava by its pre-war name Pressburg). After Strasbourg he visited Paris and London. *The London Jewish Chronicle* [17] on 8 March 1924 reported the following: "Deputy Rabbi Meir Shapiro, of Sanok, Poland, has arrived in London to collect funds in behalf of the *Keren Hatorah* of Agudat Israel." On the 15 of March 1924 the same newspaper printed a correction: 'We are asked to state that Deputy Rabbi Meir Shapiro, of Sanok, Poland, came to this country in the interest of the Lublin World Yeshivah, and not , as reported last week, to collect funds on behalf of the *Keren Hatora* of the Agudat Israel. The Lublin Yeshiva is independent of any particular section or party'.

The construction of the magnificent building of the Yeshivah started in 1926. The Yeshivah was officially opened on 24 June 1930. It was a modern school with good living conditions for the students. Its library had one of the most impressive collections of rabbinical literature, largely donated by Meir Shapiro himself. In his article [13] kept in the Archive of the Sejm Prof. Paul B. Fenton quotes the following confession which Rabbi Shapiro with heavy premonition made to Rabbi Moshe Blau after the realisation of his project:

> At the moment when my idea of establishing the Central World Yeshivah was accomplished I regret that it was not at that time an intelligent, insightful person who would have suggested to me that it would be better to build this Yeshivah in *Eretz Israel* (the Land of Israel) instead of this building. I had invested all my strength and all my life in Diaspora. Who can predict what will happen in future to all of this?

As already mentioned, the second great idea proposed by Rabbi Meir Shapiro at the World Conference of Agudat Israel in 1923 was the *Daf Yomi* Talmud study programme [8]. He participated only in the ceremonial conclusion of the first seven- and-a-half-year cycle of *Daf Yomi* in 1931. The 11th *Siyum* took place on 1 March 2005 all over the world, from USA to Russia. In United Kingdom thousands of people took part in the *Siyum* in London, Manchester and other cities. It is remarkable that the celebration also took place in the building of the former Yeshivah Chachmei Lublin from were the proceedings were transmitted by satellite all over the world. In every place where the *Siyum* was celebrated the participants acknowledged that the *Daf Yomi* was the idea of Rabbi Meir Shapiro and that due to his wisdom the programme he proposed is uniting Jewish people on all continents.

The personality of Rabbi Shapiro will continue to attract attention of scholars and, undoubtedly, the documents kept in the Polish archives, which have now became accessible, will assist the research of his future biographers.

Notes and References

1. *Parliament Rzeczypospolitei Polskiej*, 1919–1927 [The Parliament of the Polish Republic 1919– 1927], [eds] professors Henryk Moscicki and Wlodzimierz Dzwonkowski, (Warsaw: L. Zlotnicki, 1928), pp. 310–311.
2. Tadeusz and Witold Rzepecki, *Sejm i Senat* [The Sejm and Senate] (Poznan: Wielcopolska Ksiegarnia Nakladowa Karola Rzepeckiego, 1923), p. 125.
3. See Chapter 3 in this book and R. Bayvel "Who was Rabbi Natan Spira?" *The Polish Review* **50**, 2 (2005), pp. 195–199.
4. M. Wunder, *Elef Margaliot* [Thousans Pearls], (Jerusalem: Institute of the History of the Jews of Galicia, 1993), p. 219.
5. Chapter 1 in this book and R. Bayvel, "Printers and Princes", *The Polish Review*, 45, 3 (2000), pp. 347–54.
6. Volhynia was a Polish province before the second partition of Poland (1793) when it became a part of the Russian Empire. Korets is a town in Volhynia.
7. Prof. Yacov Guggenheim, Institute of Contemporary Jewry, the Hebrew University, Jerusalem, letter to the author, 9 December 2001.
8. Database of the Archive of the Sejm, the Library of the Sejm, Warsaw, Poland.
9. Dr Wojciech Kulisiewicz, Director of the Library of the Sejm, letter to the author, 14 January 2000.
10. *Encyclopaedia Judaica*, vol. 14, p. 1299.
11. *The Encyclopaedia of Hasidism*, [ed.] Tzvi M. Rabinovicz (Northvale and London: Jason Aronson, 1996), p. 448–449.
12. *The Shorter Jewish Encyclopaedia*, (Jerusalem: Hebrew University, 1994), vol. 4, p. 999.
13. Prof. P.B. Fenton, *Il ya 70 ans un Rabbin hasidique a Strasbourg* (70 years since the visit of the Hasidic Rabbi to Strasbourg), Almanach K.K.L. (Strasbourg, 1995), pp. 35–41.
14. Dr. Wojciech Kulisiewicz, Director of the Library of the Sejm, letter to the author, 8 October 2004.
15. J. Webber, UNESCO Professor of Jewish and Interfaith studies, University of Birmingham, personal communication.
16. *Archiwum Akt Nowych* (The Archive of New Documents, Warsaw), Archive of the Ministry of Foreign Affairs, (1918–1939), Warsaw,

Department of Politic and Economics, file 7976, survey of Jewish press (1923–1924), sheet 66, 26 July 1924, Political life.
17. *The Jewish Chronicle*, London, 8 and 15 March 1924.

5

A Rebel and a Victim - The Life and Work of Chava Shapiro

Originally published in The Jewish Quarterly,
vol. 50, issue 3, 2003, pp 101-106

In 1985 Naomi Caruso, the librarian of a Jewish public library in Montreal, Canada, found a bundle of 184 letters carefully tied with a ribbon. The bundle was in the archive of a well-known Jewish writer and journalist, Reuven Brainin (1862-1939), who died in New York.

In 1941 his sons deposited the archive in the library because it was their father who had established it. Nobody looked at the letters for 44 years. Caruso discovered that they were love letters written (in Hebrew) to Reuven Brainin by a woman called Chava Shapiro over a period of 29 years (1899-1928). In order to find out more about her, Caruso sent a short note to an Israeli newspaper under the title 'Who was Chava Shapiro?' In response, a former compatriot of Shapiro's who was a friend of her son published an article in which he explained that Chava came from the Ukraine (then part of the Russian Empire) and that she was one of the first women in the history of Hebrew literature and journalism. Continuing her research[1], Caruso found out that, apart from writing books and articles, Shapiro had kept a diary for more than 40 years (1899-1941), now in an archive in Israel. There is an entry on Chava Shapiro in the Dictionary of Modem Hebrew Literature (Tel Aviv, 1965-7).

My personal interest in her came from the fact that she was my great aunt (a sister of my grandfather), which prompted me to do additional research in several countries. It is now possible to reconstruct her life, which was strongly affected by the events and upheavals in Europe in the twentieth century, from family and friends' recollections and her diary and letters to Reuven Brainin. One could even imagine an exciting film based on her story.

Chava Shapiro was born in 1876 in Slavuta (a small town in the Pale of Settlement in Ukraine, then in the Russian Empire). Her ancestors were printers who left an important religious heritage. Her father was a very successful businessman and one of the leading citizens of his community. In spite of her exceptional abilities, she received no formal education at a time when marriage was the only destiny of a Jewish girl. It was thanks to her mother that she received privately some secular education. Her mother loved Hebrew and passed this love on to her children, who all spoke the language. Chava was married by the age of 18 to a husband from a well-to-do family of bankers. This was an arranged marriage, as was customary at the time. Two years later, a son was born, and Chava and her family moved to Warsaw. They were very well off, owned a summer house in a suburb and often vacationed at various spas in Europe. It was around then that she realized she did not love her husband. In 1899 she began writing her diary, which forms a kind of interior monologue. She was lonely and unsuccessfully tried to adapt to the role of conventional wife. Her diary became a means of survival and, in later life, a substitute for the family and close friends she had lost.

At the same time Chava began to feel more and more frustrated by the life of the Jewish bourgeoisie to which she belonged, and her diary expressed her dissatisfaction with an existence devoid of ideas. She complained of the mediocrity and small-minded people who surrounded her. (Her biggest fear was that the longer she remained among them, the more she would come to resemble them.) One entry reads:

> Give me life, space, light, freedom! I am choking! Alas, how petty, impoverished, sad and small life is if it only consists of daily worries, small matters that only deal with the needs of the hour. How glorious and grand life can be when it consists of an inner world filled with spiritual uplift, mental aspirations and great deeds! I experience strong feeling, of power that give me courage to resist and rebel. I wish with all my heart and soul, with all my strength and might to break out, to remove my bonds, to be strong so I can escape my prison, break down the chains, shatter and destroy them and reach for freedom and open spaces.

In 1899, while staying at an Austrian resort with her mother, Chava met a friend of her parents called Reuven Brainin. He was a well-known writer and literary critic and one of the leading intellectuals of his day. He was a friend of many Zionist leaders, attended all the Zionist Congresses (including the first one in Basel) and later published the first biography of Theodor Herzl. His writing and frequent public lectures all over Europe made him popular, especially amongst the young Eastern European Jews for whom he was a role model.

Reuven was 16 years older than Chava, a married man and father of four children. He lived in beautiful apartments, dressed fashionably, travelled widely and collected books and works of art. But although he was a well-known writer, his work did not provide sufficient means for him and his family to live in the style to which he was accustomed. When he had money, he spent it lavishly; when he did not, he complained to his friends and was not averse to begging for loans, which he seldom repaid. After knowing Chava for a little more than a year he asked her too for money. To make ends meet, his wife worked as a masseuse in the fashionable spas of Europe, binding her husband to her more securely than their marital bonds ever could have done.

Chava met Reuven just at the time when she was searching for some solution to her private misery. Meeting him, falling in love and starting an affair, in fact, served to increase her anger and frustration at having to live a life that was not of her own choosing. Reuven was the catalyst she needed to prompt her into action. She wanted him to be her lover and best friend as well as role model and mentor, demands which Reuven found impossible to fulfil. He was then at the height of his career and success. Meeting him changed Chava's life forever. Brainin introduced her to the literary milieu in Warsaw, where she met I. L. Peretz, a classic scholar of Yiddish and Hebrew literature; D. Frishman, a prominent writer and literary critic; and later the famous poet Ch. N. Bialik. Peretz and Frishman noticed her exceptional abilities, took a special interest in ·her and encouraged to start writing. Chava later acknowledged in her diary the help she received from Peretz, who spent a lot of time teaching her creative writing. Her first story, 'The Rose', was published in 1902. Her book of 15 stories called 'Collection of Sketches' (1908) became an important literary event because there were so few Jewish women writers at the time.

Feminism was one of the most important issues of her life. She started to promote her feminist views even in her early stories, expressing her feelings of frustration at a male-dominated world that did everything to discourage young women's desire for independence. In the Introduction to the above-mentioned book, Chava wrote: 'Our literature is missing the participation of one half of the human race, that of the weaker sex. My most fervent wish is that members of my sex will awaken and follow in my footsteps. Our literature will remain impoverished and colourless as long as women will not take an active part in it'. She continued to assert such feminist views in her later articles.

In 1899 Chava and Reuven started a correspondence that lasted for 29 years, mostly one-sided. Whilst Chava was still married she had to keep her letter-writing secret and Reuven's letters had to be sent to post offices where Chava (or a trusted go-between) could pick them up. After 1903, when she left her husband, his letters were addressed directly to her. Reuven, however, remained married to a very watchful wife whom Chava nicknamed 'the policeman'. (Sometimes, to fool Reuven's wife, Chava used the male gender in the text of her letters and signed them with her mother's maiden name.)

From the time she became involved with Reuven, Chava realized that she had to change her life, regardless of consequences, and so began plotting her escape. In one of her letters, she points out that when she met him, she was a modest wig-wearing Jewish religious woman, for whom an adulterous affair with a married man was a cardinal sin. Reuven, however, was a confirmed ladies' man, only looking for a short-term flirtation, and did not expect that their association would open an emotional floodgate. When, in 1903, Chava told Reuven that she intended to leave her husband, he immediately grew alarmed, advising caution and further reflection. In response, she wrote to him:

> I can see, my darling, that I am all alone and have no one at my side. Still, I feel brave and ready to do whatever is necessary. Let me explain. when you advised me to give up and go back to my husband, I was shocked. Those were the very words I thought I would never ever hear from you. It made me realize that you, too, my only hope and comfort, will not stand by me. Yet in spite of that I shall not give up. On the contrary, I shall continue to fight with greater determination. First I must study and further my development. I feel I have enough strength to achieve my goal, which is to throw off the bonds that others have placed on me. The time is ripe. I have suffered and waited for six years, but no more. All I have to do is find enough resolve within myself. I shall go on fighting and win my freedom!

The same year Chava left her husband and returned to her parents. The price of her freedom was high. She was forced to leave her beloved six-year-old son with his father. Although Chava's initial hopes that Reuven would provide her with love and security were quashed early in their relationship, she nevertheless kept on hoping that somehow the two of them would eventually live together. She was convinced it was their destiny. In a letter to Brainin in 1904, she wrote:

This love of mine is growing and expanding and requires words which my Hebrew vocabulary lacks. Brainin, how can I live without you when I handed over to you my soul and all my inner goodness? Everyone around us is so petty and foolish, always conspiring ... But you, my love, are so different, you are the best, aren't you? Tell me, my darling, that I have to trust you in everything, tell me! It seems to me that I have never loved you or been as devoted to you as since our last encounter. Reuven, why did you take my soul ... My darling, you have realized that my love is bottomless – you said so yourself.

In 1907 Chava wrote to Reuven that her divorce had been finalized, her dowry returned and custody of her son granted to her. She felt enormous joy at her sense of freedom. In her next letter she mentioned that she had found a wonderful apartment and lives as befits a 'rich lady', 'so you have to treat me with respect now that I have become rich. I know that you like the rich, so obviously you like rich women.'

Chava felt that her route to independence lay in a proper education. She went to study in Austria and then Switzerland, where in 1910 she received a doctorate in philosophy. She became a professional writer and journalist. She acquired a wide knowledge of literature, art, history and psychology and was fluent in nine languages. Her articles in various journals reflected her exceptional erudition, as well as the crystal-clear logic and sharpness of mind with which she analysed current political. issues. She always managed to bring some original insight to the subjects she wrote about. She was also a brilliant and persuasive conversationalist and went on publishing stories in several journals.

While travelling on journalistic assignments Chava continued to see Reuven. During her studies she met several eligible men whom she quite liked but who lost their appeal when Reuven chose to reappear. Several times it seemed that the emotional attachment was gone and that they would go their separate ways but, rather than let that happen, it was Reuven who relit the flame and reawakened Chava's passion. Whenever he felt frustrated with the way his own life was going, he would turn to the only person who had always believed in his greatness and who adored him unconditionally, and who was also young and pretty – Chava. All he needed to do when he was becoming depressed was drop a few lines to Chava, pushing the right emotional buttons. It never failed. No matter how bitterly she objected to his tactics, she fell under his spell again and again. Chava hoped to pin Reuven down to a more stable relationship and, no matter how deviously he dealt with her, refused to admit that he had no intention of leaving his wife.

In November 1910, Brainin and his family moved to Canada when he became the editor of a newspaper in Montreal. When he had seen Chava in May 1910 he had not told her about his intentions, so discovering accidentally while reading the newspaper that Reuven had settled in Canada was a terrible blow. For the next three years (1910-13) there was little communication between Reuven and Chava. But, just when it seemed that she had her life under control, Reuven turned up unexpectedly. He arrived in 1913 to spend four months in Europe, the last of them with Chava, the longest and most intense time the lovers had spent together since their meeting fourteen years earlier. However, after the two months of ecstasy were over, Reuven returned to Canada, promising to write letters twice a week. Chava received only two letters – and then there was complete silence. Initially she was convinced that Brainin could not write to her because of his wife and thought of him as a victim. Shmuel Horodetsky (their closest friend, and a distinguished historian) tried in vain to persuade her that it was she, and not Brainin, who was the victim. In her diary she wrote:

> Horodetsky thinks that I am Brainin's victim. For 15 years he has held me in his net and does not let me go. How much truth is there in this? Is he my personal disaster, pushing me off the straight road and preventing me from ever reaching a safe haven? Do I have to remove his chains to prove to myself that what Horodetsky sees is right?

Chava continued to write to Brainin even if she did not get any replies. She begged him for a letter: 'I am made of flesh and blood and your insulting behaviour poisons my blood. I cannot believe that you can be so cruel towards me.' In her desperation she contemplated killing herself and sent Brainin a letter that she intended as a suicide note. In another letter she writes:

'I hear your voice, see your eyes, feel your hand caressing mine, you are so near to me I shudder, it is like dreaming while I am awake.'

In May 1914 Chava received two letters from Brainin, the last he ever wrote to her (although she continued to write to him on a regular basis until 1920).

When the First World War broke out in 1914 Chava left Germany because otherwise she would have been interned, and returned home to her mother (her father had died in 1912) and son, who had stayed with his grandparents after the divorce. She lived in Slavuta for several years. Even during the war Chava continued to write letters to Brainin. They usually corresponded in Hebrew, but among the collection of her letters in the Montreal library there are three written in Russian in 1916 (at one stage during the war the Russian government accused Jews of spying for Germany and Austro-Hungary and so correspondence in Hebrew and Yiddish was forbidden).

During her life in Slavuta a close friendship developed between Chava and a local man who worked as a forester on the estate of a rich landowner. The forester, a Czech by nationality, was a tall, good-looking but lonely bachelor, who lived in a house at the edge of the forest. In Slavuta Jews were not accustomed to such a relationship between a woman from a religious family and a gentile man. There were even rumours that Chava had an affair with the forester. Whatever the truth of this, her friendship may later have saved the life of Chava and her son.

Her life was obviously affected by the events in Russia in 1917-19: the February revolution in 1917, when Tsar Nicholas II was overthrown; the short period of democracy; the Bolshevik revolution in October 1917; the German occupation of parts of Russia in 1918; and the Civil War. During a short period after the February revolution Chava was very enthusiastic because she thought that the revolution would bring freedom and equality to Jews. She was elected as a representative from her town to the local legislature. As she wrote in her diary:

> Almost two months have passed since the big changes have occurred in Russia ... Even the most enthusiastic dreamers did not expect such a big transformation – such a revolution will spur every living person who is capable of understanding social life, to work toward an awakening. There is new life everywhere. life that is filled with demands and aspirations for new light. And our own world is filled with joy and freedom, hopes and aspirations ... My hands are filled with work. Revolution, upheavals, change after change. Life is filled with interest, with work, grief and worry but the intoxication of triumph too ... Even in this small town one cannot excuse oneself from community work. The day before yesterday I returned from Kiev (the capital of the Ukraine). This is the third time since the summer that I have visited there. I spent several weeks there, and there too life is filled with work.

After the Bolshevik revolution Chava became disillusioned and withdrew from politics. During 1918-19 power in the Ukraine changed almost every day. But whoever was in charge (the Whites, the Reds, warlords of every kind or simply bandits), all of them started their period of rule with pogroms against the Jews. Tens of thousands of Jews were murdered, wounded, raped and robbed. There are several entries in Chava's diary where she described the situation in Slavuta, 'Pogroms are raging everywhere, every person in Slavuta has been under a constant death threat'. She herself had to hide in a stranger's home for a whole week. In July she wrote:

'Before the angel of death descends upon us, there is only one concern: to save oneself in any way possible.' When the Red Army temporarily retreated from Slavuta in August 1919, Chava and her son – with the help of her Czech friend – managed to escape to Czechoslovakia. When she arrived in Prague her first letter was written to Brainin:

'My dear old friend, I am alive, I am alive! I and my son have escaped by some miracles from the jaws of death.'

This, along with the other letters, went unanswered. In the same year Chava sent several articles to a Jewish journal in New York about her experiences in the Ukraine, although she asked for them to be published anonymously in order not to endanger her family who had stayed behind. In one of her unanswered letters to Brainin she asked how much they knew in the USA about the suffering of Jews in the Ukraine. Chava pleaded with him, 'Do all you can to save our miserable brothers there, their life is in danger.' In another letter she wrote, 'I lost contact with my family in Slavuta when the Reds returned.' At the same time she emphasizes that the main reason for her suffering is Brainin's behaviour towards her, which is "dishonourable and indecent." 'My present pain is worse than what I suffered during the worst period of the pogroms, when I came face to face with beasts.'

In 1920 Chava heard that Brainin had been in Europe but had not contacted her. After that she stopped writing to him. Chava's son started studying engineering in Prague and for a short period of time she also lived there. Her mother and other family lived in the Ukraine, which became part of the Soviet Union. The family business and property were confiscated by the Soviet authorities. Therefore, for the first time in her life, she had to work to support herself and her son. In one of the entries in her diary for 1923 she wrote:

I am still relatively young and could be of help. But I refuse to be a burden on anyone. My son is finishing his studies and I would like so much to go to Palestine, be among friends who are close to my heart, work, be active, help others, but my hands are tied. Without money it is not possible and here I am choking ... I have nothing, no life, no friends, no relatives. If this is my fate, I must fight it!

Chava's Czech friend lived in a small provincial town, Mukachevo, and she decided to accept his invitation to move there. She stayed there for four years. The entries in her diary about her friend are very warm.

> From the heavens I was sent this goy friend. Without his help, it is certain that I and my son would not have been saved two years ago in Russia. If it were not for him, my life here would be much harder. I owe him so much. I must admit that I have never met, even within our own people, a man with so much heart, who thinks that no sacrifice is too great and who only thinks of others, never of himself.

She continued working as a journalist, writing numerous articles for German, Czech and Jewish newspapers and journals in several countries, sometime under the name Eva Shapiro. In 1925 she interviewed the President of Czechoslovakia, Thomas Masaryk (and in 1935 published a book about him). Life was comfortable for her in Mukachevo, but she could not live without the intellectual atmosphere of Prague and in 1925 she moved back there. She immediately discovered that it was very difficult to make a living from the proceeds of her journalistic activities and desperately tried to find other sources of income, but in vain. She was particularly upset that even her application to become a teacher of Hebrew in a Jewish school was rejected. Her personal life was no better. In 1925, while attending a Zionist congress in Austria, Chava met Brainin for the first time since they had parted in 1913, but he avoided all personal contact with her. Chava's only letter to Brainin after 1920 was written on her fiftieth birthday, 21 December 1928:

> A quarter of a century ago, when you were in great financial difficulty, you turned to me with a request for money. I sent you 200 roubles and never mentioned the matter again until this day. Times have changed and I find myself in the same predicament. I am forced to remind you. Brainin, do not delay!

Brainin again did not reply. This was the end of their 29-year correspondence. Brainin died in 1939. It seems that Chava's letters accompanied him through his many travels in different countries and that he kept them until his death.

Around 1926 Chava became emotionally involved with a new man called Josef Winternitz, also an intellectual, a scion of one of the most respected Czech-Jewish families. She was attracted to him, respected and admired him. She knew she was getting involved with someone with behavioural peculiarities, but she hoped he would change under her influence. As she wrote in her diary, 'This is not the right choice, but life is so meaningless without an emotional commitment.' In 1930 she agreed to marry Josef in the hope of finding long-sought peace, security, permanence and a more conventional life. Yet, this second marriage was a disaster from the very beginning. Her husband had a twisted paranoiac personality and turned her life into a nightmare existence.

The home that Chava was hoping to establish for herself gradually became hell. As Europe was becoming increasingly dangerous for Jews, Chava was able to send her son to the USA in 1937. She was sending away the only person she loved, not knowing if she would see him again. In 1939 the Nazis occupied Czechoslovakia and in 1941 they started the deportation of Jews to concentration camps. Chava was afraid that she could be deported any day and that her diary would perish with her. The last entry was made in 1941:

> For more than 40 years I have made entries in this diary. It has become part of my soul. I haven't written Hebrew for the last two years and now I take my leave of this diary too and hand it over to some strangers. My son is overseas, and who knows where I am going? My people's fate is mine too. A month ago I was still full of life, how I hoped, as I shall go on hoping, to see my son again. Now I am very weak, yet I have still so much to endure! My son, my son, let him be happy in his life. God take him and look after him! It is so difficult to bid farewell, even from a diary, even from this lifeless piece of paper that breathed the same air as I, who used to write in it.

The diary survived the war but its author did not. It somehow found its way to Chava's brother in Palestine. He deposited it at the Machon Genazim (Bio Bibliographic Institute), Tel Aviv, in 1956. It is stated in all published accounts of Shapiro's life that she was deported to Terezin and died there. But documents reveal that she (under the name Eva Winternitz) and her husband Josef were due to be deported from Prague to Terezin with the transport 'Cv' on 6 March 1943. Yet, Chava died in Prague before that deportation took place, on 28 February. Her husband was deported and died in Terezin on 18 March 1944. After the war, when her friends, writers and journalists discovered she had died, they published many tributes to this talented woman.

Interest in Chava's life and work has increased since the discovery of her letters to Brainin, and her writings have become the subject of research in several universities. Her contribution to Hebrew literature and journalism is substantial, but she could have achieved much more if she had lived in different times and circumstances. Her diary and letters to Brainin have great historical and literary value and are arguably her finest works. They deserve to be translated into English and published in full, so that the name of Chava Shapiro is not forgotten.

References

1.   "Chava Shapiro : a woman before her time", Naomi Caruso, MA Thesis, Department of Jewish Studies, McGill University, 1991

Siddur (daily prayer book) *Seder avodah u-moreh derekh*, according to the Hasidic rite (minhag Sefard). Printed in Slavuta by Rabbi Shmuel Avraham Shapiro, 1827-1828. Credit: Sotheby's.

Siddur, *Seder tefillat nehora*, according to the Ashkenazic rite (minhag Ashkenaz). Printed in Slavuta by Rabbi Shmuel Avraham Shapiro, 1832-1833. Credit: Sotheby's.

1.1. St Dorothy's, the Sanguszko family church, the only surviving part of the palace in Slavuta. The Polish inscription reads: 'St Dorothy Pray for Us'. Credit: Rachel Bayvel, 1972

2.1. The title page of the book *Tikunei HaZohar*, published by the Shapiros in 1865 in Zhitomir reads, 'In the printing house of the partners, the grandchildren of the Rabbi of Slavuta. Chanina-Lipa and Yehoshua-Heshel Shapiro. In Zhitomir [Hebrew]. Sefer Tikunei HaZohar, Zhitomir, in the Printing House of L. and H. Shapiro [Russian]'.

הסכמה

דן מחותני הרי"ש ובש"ק הגביר המפורסים כבוד ה"ר יהושע העשיל שי' מבשר ואמר
במכתבו אלי · אשר השיגו רשיון מהצענזר להעלות על מכבש דפום ספרי זהר
ותקונים עם זהרא חדש שנית · כי מרוב חבת הקדש הראשונים דפום סלאוויטא אזרו ואלה
ואינם מצוים כ"כ · והמלאכה הזתה דים ליפות ולהדר עבודת הקדש בריבו הוצאה · ע"כ
מבקש שלא יבולע להקדש בנזק משיני נבול ח"ו · אמרתי ישר · כי הלא נודע בשערים יקר
תפארת דפום מחותניי היקרים הבש"קק שי" אשר זכו לאותיות מאירות עינים · וגם מנחתם
להסיר סיני טעיות הדפום עד מקום שידם מגעת לטובה · כפי אשר זכו מאבותיהם הקרושים
ומעשה אבותיהם בידיהם · כן נודע אשר נמנו וגמרו גאוני קרמאי ובתראי להסב איסור השגת
נבול גם בהדפסת ספרי קרש · לכן אשנה · ואשלש גם אנכי לאמר בבקשה שלא ישיגו נבול
מחותני המדפיסים בהדפסת ספרי קרש הנ"ל משך עשרה שנים מיום כלות הדפום בלי שם
ערמה ומרמה בעולם · ומבטחוני אשר אהב" י יקיימו מה שקבלו כבר מרגאונים כאמר אמים ·
בגלל זאת יברך ה' אותם באורך ימים ושנים טובים · וייטיב ה' להם בגו"ר בבני חיי ומזוני
רויחא אכי"ר · באתי עה"ח ביום א' שלשה עשר ימים לחדש סיון תרכ"ג לפ"ק :

נאום אהרן בהרב המפורסים מוה' מרדכי זצוקללה"ה מטשרנאביל

3.1. HRH Prince Charles, The Prince of Wales at the tombstone of Rabbi Natan Spira at the Old Jewish cemetery in Kazimierz, Krakow (Poland) in June 2002. Credit: PA Images/Alamy Stock Photo.

4.1. Students of Yeshiva Chachmei Lublin with Rabbi Meir Shapiro, c.1930. Credit: Grodzka Gate – NN Theatre Centre.

5.1. Chava Shapiro, inscribed 'To Reuben Brainin - Chava Shapiro. Chol hamoed sukkot 5674 (October 1913), Berlin'. Courtesy of the Chava Shapiro fonds, Jewish Public Library, Montreal, Canada.

5.2. Chava Shapiro, portrait as a postcard, sent to Reuben Brainin in Montreal, Canada from Slavuta, 1914. Credit: Chava Shapiro fonds, Jewish Public Library, Montreal, Canada.

5.3. Postcard portrait of Reuben Brainin in 1898. Credit: Photograph Collection, Jewish Public Library, Montreal, Canada.

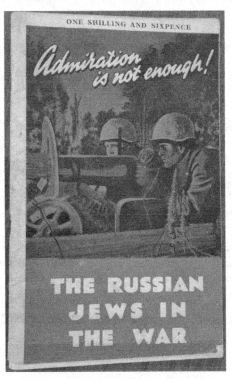

7.1. Booklet cover 'The Russian Jews in the War' produced in honour of the visit of Solomon Mikhoels and Itzik Fefer to London.

7.2. Solomon Mikhoels and Itzik Fefer, commemorative booklet of their visit to London 1943, see 7.4.

7.3. Solomon Mikhoels and Itzik Fefer in Moscow, 1943, before their historic visit to the West, used in the promotional material for their visit in Manchester, 1943.

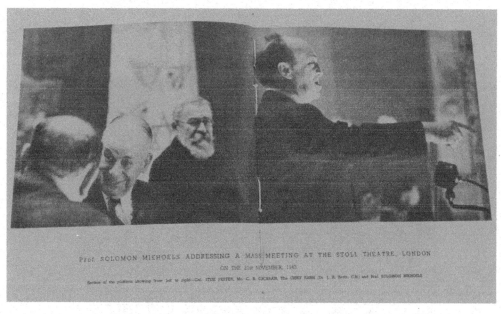

7.4. Prof Solomon Mikhoels addressing a meeting in the presence of the Chief Rabbi Dr J. H. Hertz from the book, 'Greetings & goodwill messages from Anglo-Jewry to Soviet Jewry in commemoration of the visit to Great Britain of Prof. Solomon Mikhoels and Col. Itzik Feffer, November 1943', London 1944.

All images in Plates 7.1–7.4 are from Prof David S Latchman's collection.

8.1. President Mannerheim with members of the Jewish Community taking part in the commemoration service at the Helsinki synagogue, 6 December 1944, presenting a wreath to the Finnish Jewish community in memory of the soldiers killed during the wars of 1939-1944. Credit: Mannerheim Museum, Helsinki

8.2. President Mannerheim, Helsinki synagogue, 6 December 1944 with members of the Finnish Jewish Community at the commemorative meeting in memory of the soldiers killed during the wars of 1939-1944. Credit: Mannerheim Museum, Helsinki

8.3. President Mannerheim, Helsinki synagogue, 6 December 1944. Credit: Mannerheim Museum, Helsinki

9.1. *Unmasked Doctor-Murderer.* A typical cartoon at the time of 'The Doctors' Plot', from a popular Soviet satirical magazine, Krokodil. Credit: *Krokodil*, January 1953

10.1. The Ketuba of Rachel Shapiro and Leopold Bayvel (Chanina Lipa ben Pinchas Ha-Levi), 1962. Credit: Bayvel family.

11a.1. *Portrait of Marc Chagall*, mid-1910s. National Art Museum of Belarus, Minsk

11.a.2. *Clockmaker*, 1914. Vitebsk Art Museum

11.a.3. *Divorce*, 1907. Vitebsk Art Museum

All images from Aleksandra Shatskikh, *Vitebsk - The Life of Art* (Yale University Press, 2007)

11.b.1. *Head of a Young Jew (self-portrait)*, 1916. State Tretyakov Gallery. Moscow

11.b.2. *V.I. Lenin speaks with the representatives of English Trade Unions.* 26 May 1920. Central Museum of V.I. Lenin, Moscow

11.b.3. *Portrait of S.M. Mikhoels*, 1927, A.A. Bakhrushin Central Theatre Museum, Moscow

11.b.4. *Self-portrait*, 1911. State Russian Museum, St Petersburg

All images from *Natan Altman*, Sovetskii khudozhnik, 1971, Moscow

11.c.1. *Portrait of A.L. Kaplan* by G.S. Vereisky, 1958, lithograph

11.c.2. *Rogachev*. Just Before the Thunderstorm, 1954, charcoal

11.c.3. *Wedding Song*, tempera, gouache

All images from '*Anatoly Lvovich Kaplan*', B. Suris, Khudozhnik RSFSR, Leningrad, 1972

6

Tales of 'Tank City'

Originally published in The Jewish Quarterly -
vol. 52, issue 2 Summer 2005

This piece was written in May 2005, marking the sixtieth anniversary of Allied victory over Nazi Germany, in memory of the Soviet Jews who produced weapons for the Allied victory.

Everybody knows about the vital contribution made by the Soviet Army in World War II. Many people are also aware that virtually all the able-bodied Jewish men living in the USSR served in this Army – more than 200,000 died in its ranks. In no other ethnic minority group were so many soldiers made Heroes of the Soviet Union (the highest military honour).

More than this, however, there were many thousands of Jewish men and women who worked behind the scenes developing and producing new tanks, planes, artillery, other weapons and ammunition. Some relocated defence installations from areas of Soviet territory that were later occupied by the Germans to the Urals and Siberia so as to build new factories there. Without the unsung efforts of such people, it would have been impossible to defeat Nazi Germany.

Almost all the individuals I am going to describe were born in the Pale of Settlement in Tsarist Russia. The 1917 October Revolution gave Jews unrestricted access to education. The younger ones craved knowledge and rushed to study in universities and institutions of high learning in the major cities. So, when Stalin embarked on a policy of industrialization, there were already many Jewish scientists and engineers who took an active part in constructing new plants and factories.

Even before the war, Jews already occupied important positions at all levels in industrial management, as People's Commissars (ministers) and their deputies, directors of factories, chief designers and so on, some of them in the defence industry. While Stalin needed them during the war, many outstanding Jews were decorated or awarded Stalin prizes. Yet, after the war he and his successors suppressed all details of the contribution of the Jews to the struggle against Nazism. It was only after the collapse of the USSR that state archives were opened, and historians given access to vital sources of information. This included historians such as Leonid Mininberg ('Soviet Jews in USSR Science and Industry during the Second World War', 1995) and, more recently, Arkadii Vaksberg ('From Hell to Paradise and Back', 2003) who carried out essential research and produced important books about the key role played by the Soviet Jews behind the lines in defeating the Nazi Germany. Yet little of this remarkable story is available in English.

I have a personal interest in this subject. My father, who joined the Soviet Army when Germany attacked the USSR in June 1941, was wounded at the Leningrad front and sent to hospital in the city for treatment. Many factories that before the war produced civilian goods became part of the military industrial effort. When my father recovered from his wounds, he was appointed a director of one such factory (where he had worked before the war). This started to produce mortars, which went straight from the factory gates to the Front.

My father remained in Leningrad during the whole 900 days of the siege. His appointment to such an important position underscores the fact that the wartime authorities turned a blind eye to the 'shortcomings' of people who were capable of organizing military production. He was not a member of the Communist Party. Indeed, he was an Orthodox Jew, as the people in power must have known, because he prayed in the Leningrad synagogue (which functioned even during the siege). He personally knew several of the Jews who had been put in charge of the biggest defence plants in Leningrad and it was from him that I first heard their names. These people became very well-known during the war and were often mentioned in the Soviet press. Yet, since their achievements were repressed and most of them have now been forgotten, I wanted to pay tribute to some of the most prominent.

Tanks

The first person I want to talk about is Isaac Zal'tsman. At the beginning of the war the Germans destroyed almost all the Soviet tanks. In 1941 Zal'tsman was the director of the Kirov tank-production factory, the largest in Leningrad. Within three months of the start of the war, even while the city was being severely bombed by the Germans, he was able to organize the production of modern tanks. My father told me that Zal'tsman was known as 'the king of tanks'. Stalin gave him the Honour of the Hero of

Socialist Labour (one of the first during the war) in September 1941. By then it was necessary to evacuate the entire factory from Leningrad to the Urals. Zal'tsman organized the transfer of all the machinery, 15,000 workers and their families to Chelyabinsk, where the machinery was left in the open air and production started immediately. Only later were walls built around the production lines. In 1942-3 Zal'tsman was the people's Commissar for the tank industry. He had the rank of major-general and was decorated many times.

When heavy fighting broke out near Moscow in autumn 1941, the army urgently needed modern tanks. The tanks had been manufactured, but they could not be sent to the Front because one small part (made at a Moscow factory) was missing. Since two planes sent to Chelyabinsk with these details had been downed by the Germans, delivery of the tanks was under threat. Zal'tsman came up with a very unusual solution. He put the tanks on a train going towards Moscow and accompanied them himself. Another train with the missing parts was sent from Moscow. The trains met somewhere on the way, the parts were transferred to the train going to Moscow and installed en route so they could be sent straight to the Front. Timely delivery of the tanks greatly contributed to the first defeat of the Germans before Moscow in December 1941.

Later, several other plants were evacuated to Chelyabinsk and consolidated into a single complex under Zal'tsman. Journalists called it the 'Tank city'. In 1942 it produced more tanks and self-propelled artillery than the whole of Germany.

Zal'tsman looked after his workers well. The plant helped some collective farms and obtained food in return. The workforce ate twice a day in the canteen, quite exceptional in those difficult times. Their children also received food. 'Tank city' incorporated a factory that supplied many thousands of its workers with garments and footwear.

Planes

Among the creators of Soviet fighter planes two chief designers, Semyon Lavochkin and Mikhail Gurevich, became famous at home and abroad. Both were awarded the Honour of Hero of Socialist Labour, won the Stalin Prizes and were decorated many times.

Semyon Lavochkin created the La-5 fighters that appeared so suddenly and unexpectedly during the Battle of Stalingrad, destroying the planes that had been sent to provide supplies for the surrounded German troops. He continued to develop new planes during the war. According to the pilots, the La-7 was one of the best fighter planes of the Second World War. Gurevich was one of the two creators of the celebrated MIG fighter planes. (In fact, in MiG, M stands for Mikoyan and G for Gurevich, although people joked that the MIG was named after Mikhail Iosifovich Gurevich). The MIG-3 fighters destroyed half the German planes during their air raids on Moscow in 1941.

Artillery

One of the best-known organizers of production of Soviet armaments was Lev Gonor. He was only 33 when he was appointed a director of one of the biggest and the best defence enterprises in the country – the 'Barrikady' factory in Stalingrad, producing cannons and mortars. These mortars were used in the street fighting in Stalingrad and other cities. When the Germans captured almost all of Stalingrad in late autumn of 1942, the 'Barrikady' engineers and workers were transferred to the Urals, where a new artillery plant was built and Gonor appointed its director. He had the rank of Major General, was decorated many times, and in 1942 awarded the Honour of the Hero of Socialist Labour. He was also a member of the Jewish Antifascist Committee, chaired by the celebrated Yiddish actor Solomon Mikhoels (later murdered on Stalin's orders) which toured the West to gain support for the Soviet war effort, see Chapter 8.

We should also mention the names of those who participated in the development of rockets and rocket launchers for the Soviet Army. Among them was the leading designer Shekhtman, who created a multiple-rocket launcher system, mounted on a lorry. Another was the scientist Leonid Shvarts who in 1942, together with the fellow-scientist Moisei Komissarchik and the engineer Yakov Shor, was awarded the Stalin prize for the 'development of a new type of weapon'. Two other young scientists, Yakov Zel'dovich and Yulii Khariton, later famous as the creators of Soviet nuclear weapons, took part in the development of the fuel for the rockets. This new type of weapon was so powerful that it became tremendously popular among Soviet soldiers. They named it 'Katyusha', after the famous pre-war song whose tune can still be heard all over the world and even in synagogues where cantors use it for certain prayers (probably not knowing that 'Katyusha' is the name of a girl who, in the original song, awaits the return of her fiancée from military service).

Boris Fitterman was the chief designer of the Stalin car plant in Moscow – the largest automobile works in the USSR. During the war, while continuing its main line of production (cars and lorries), the plant also started to produce various kinds of mortars and submachine guns. The weapon designers headed by Fitterman made substantial improvements to the design of the mortars, and he often went to the Front to test the new weapons directly in battle conditions. He was awarded the Lenin Order for this in 1943.

Fitterman organized the production of more than a million submachine guns without cutting back on other important items. After the defeat of the Germans before Moscow in 1941, the Soviet Army captured 18,000 cars and trucks. Fitterman and his team of engineers managed to repair these vehicles so they could be sent back to the front. What added to the importance of this was that general production of new cars had been substantially decreased while existing plants were relocated to the East. For all his work during the war Fitterman was awarded the Stalin prize in 1945.

Ammunition

Boris Vannikov was the People's Commissar for armaments from 1939 but, together with many high-ranking Army officers, was arrested in 1941. When the war started, he was in the main state security prison. Yet, he managed to send Stalin his plans for relocating the defence industry to the East. In July 1941 he was released from prison, on Stalin's orders, and appointed First Deputy People's Commisar and (from 1942) People's Commissar for ammunition. It was under Vannikov's command that the USSR in 1942 produced more (and probably higher quality) ammunition than Germany. Yet Vannikov's health was poor, attributed by his deputy to the beatings Vannikov had received in prison.

Construction

In April 1942, when Leningrad was surrounded by German troops, there was only enough petrol in the city to last for 30 to 40 days. Attempts to deliver fuel by water failed because the Germans sunk the boats. At this critical moment Semyon Blank, a high-ranking officer in the Soviet Army, proposed the laying of a pipeline on the bed of the Ladoga Lake. This was the first time a pipeline of this length was constructed in the USSR. The chief engineer was David Shinberg. During the whole construction period of a month and a half it was bombed by the Germans. Yet, it was completed and operational for twenty months, permitting petrol to be supplied to the army and navy on the Leningrad front as well as to the city under siege.

The Wider Picture

Altogether, some 180,000 Jews – scientists, engineers, managers and workers – were decorated for the development and production of weaponry and the construction of military factories (my father among them), more than 200 of them with the Lenin Order. Twelve Jews became the Heroes of Socialist Labour. Almost 300 received the Stalin Prizes (15 per cent of those awarded). And more than 50 – directors and managers in industry, construction and transport – were promoted to the rank of General. However, few of these people were able to enjoy peace and tranquillity for the rest of their days unmolested. After the war Stalin launched the ferocious attack on the Jews which continued until his death. Mass dismissals began in 1947. Among the first to be affected were the skilled and often celebrated people who had received the highest awards for their achievements during the war. Those who lost only their jobs were the lucky ones; many were also deprived of their freedom. My father was one who lost his job. He was forced to resign from his position as director of a factory and had to work until his retirement as an ordinary engineer in the textile industry.

The wider fate of the former leaders of the Soviet war industry emerges clearly from what happened to three of the most prominent. Lev Gonor was arrested in 1952 and accused of espionage and links with the Jewish Anti-fascist Committee. He was tortured during interrogation and, for the rest of his life, suffered from the damage done to his health. Only the death of Stalin saved him. Hundreds of Jewish engineers and workers were arrested in Moscow in 1950. A particularly cruel blow fell on the Jews working at the Stalin car plant after Golda Meir, then Israel's Ambassador in Moscow, met the Jewish workers and was photographed with them. The chief designer, Boris Fitterman, was accused of espionage and an attempt to blow up the plant on the orders of American Zionists. When he asked the interrogator to produce evidence, the interrogator explained to him (as if to a child) that he was a Jew, and therefore no evidence was needed. He was sentenced to 25 years of hard labour and was released only after the death of Stalin.

The life of Isaac Zal'tsman was also dramatic. He had sometimes been described in wartime newspapers as 'the saviour of the Motherland' because, in the most difficult conditions, he had organized the production of heavy tanks – without which it would have not been possible to continue the war. Although he was a People's Commissar, the director of the largest tank factory, a deputy of the Supreme Soviet (Soviet parliament) and a Hero of Socialist Labour, he was simply thrown out like a lemon that had been squeezed dry. In 1949 he was dismissed from his position as director of the Chelyabinsk tractor plant and expelled from the Communist Party. With great difficulty he managed to find a job as foreman in a small provincial factory and then he lost even this job. He later worked as an ordinary worker, hiding his earlier titles. After many struggles, he eventually managed to return to Leningrad, where he lived before the war, and find work with a small building company decorating flats. Only in 1956 did he become director of a tool-making factory.

Many Soviet Jews, whose selfless work helped defeat Nazi Germany, were almost forgotten for more than 40 years, and practically erased from history. Although diligent research has now recovered their achievements, most of it is still only available in Russian. As we celebrated the sixtieth anniversary of Allied victory in the Second World War in 2005, it is only right that we should remember the soldiers of the Red Army (including hundreds of thousands of Jews) who put their lives on the line and bore the brunt of the fighting. But perhaps it is also time to recall those who, far from the battlefield, provided them with the essential weapons.

7

Dashed Hopes – the Story of the Jewish Anti-Fascist Committee

Originally Published in the Jewish Quarterly vol. 54, issue 2, 2007, pp 59-63

The summer of 2007 marked the fifty-fifth anniversary of the execution of the 13 members of the *Jewish Anti-Fascist Committee*, some of whom had been sent by Stalin to the West to rally the international Jewish support for the Soviet war effort. This article describes the doomed mission of Stalin's Jewish Anti-Fascist Committee (JAC) to London in 1943.

The broad outlines of the story are well known, but I recently came across a rare copy of a booklet called *The Russian Jews in the War*. Now a collector's item, this is little over a hundred pages long and was published in London in 1943 by the Jewish Fund for Soviet Russia to mark the visit of the JAC Chairman, the Jewish actor Solomon Mikhoels and the well-known Yiddish poet, Itzik Fefer. Their visit to the West was remarkable as the first – and only – occasion under Stalin when contacts between Soviet and Western Jews were not only permitted but actually *encouraged* by the Soviet state. The booklet is fascinating for the expression of views which are utterly surprising to anyone who had lived as a Jew in the former USSR. It also captures vividly the precise nature of the hopes which were raised by the JAC mission to the West, only to be so cruelly dashed. All quotations which appear in this article are taken directly from *The Russian Jews in the War*.

In his Foreword, the President of the Jewish Fund, Dr Redcliffe N. Salaman, FRS, wrote:

> This booklet gives an idea of what the Jews in Russia are doing and suffering in the war for civilization. The sacrifices which the Russians have made for the common cause are immensely greater than anything we have been called upon to make. The British people recognize their responsibility of helping the Russian Army with the

medical supplies and the equipment which they need so badly. That is the object of Mrs Clementine Churchill's Fund with which the Jewish Fund is linked. The Jews in England have special reasons for helping and for giving with greatest generosity because of what the Soviet Union has done and is doing to save the Jewish people.

The Chairman of the Appeal Committee, Lord Nathan of Churt, called upon Jews of Britain:

> The question has been asked, why should there be a Jewish Fund for Soviet Russia? I can answer that question: what appears to me is that here we have the Red Army which has put up a great and gallant fight against the Nazis, against our common foe, and, we are filled with admiration for its brave soldiers and we want to help them. We want to make a gesture of support and gratitude. Mrs Churchill started her 'Aid to Russia Fund' for this purpose. It needs more support. 'We want to contribute to it and we want to make a Jewish contribution', Mrs Churchill has asked of the Jews of Britain'.

Mrs Clementine Churchill sent the following message to the Jewish Fund in July 1943:

> I endorse everything that has been said about the feelings of the Jews of Britain and throughout the world in regard to this war against Hitler and in regard to the brave and the magnificent fight which the Russian people are making. We must do our utmost to assist them. Will you please pass to the members of your Committee and to all who have contributed my deep appreciation of their warm cooperation and help in answer to my Appeal for 'Aid to Russia'.

The activities of the Jewish Fund were also greatly supported by the spiritual leaders of the Jewish community. For example, the Chief Rabbi of the British Empire, Dr J. H. Hertz, issued the following instruction to all Jewish Ministers on the occasion of the Red Army Day, 23 February 1943:

> The religious heads in this country have suggested to their Churches that prayers be offered next Sunday for the continued success of our Russian Allies in their magnificent resistance to the murderous aggressor. The sons and daughters of Anglo-Jewry more than share these friendly feelings towards the people of Russia. I therefore direct

that the full war prayer be recited in the ordinary Sunday morning service before Aleinu. There shall be, in addition to the full war prayer a special reference in the sermon to the fact that the Battle of Britain is being fought on the Russian front, and the speaker should pray for the victory of the Russian Forces in the prayer, following his pulpit address. Offerings and donations might be made to the Jewish Fund for Soviet Russia and forwarded to Lord Nathan.

The creation of the Jewish Anti-Fascist Committee

It was the dangerous military situation at the beginning of the war that forced Stalin to put forward a scheme designed to exert influence on the world Jewry. He probably believed that Western Jews could provide financial aid and pressure their governments into opening a second front in Europe against the Nazis. These considerations prompted him to form the Jewish Anti-Fascist Committee (JAC) in April 1942. Among its members were the leading Soviet Jewish scientists, writers, actors, physicians and military men who distinguished themselves in the fight against fascism. The Chairman, Solomon Mikhoels, the great Jewish actor and head of the world-famous Moscow Yiddish Theatre, sent a message in the name of all Soviet Jews to the Jewish Fund for Soviet Russia when he asked:

> Where are you, the Jews of Britain and America? How will you repay the Nazi enemy for their inhuman atrocities against your people? It may have been your own kin, your own family whom you left behind in Russia whom the Nazis have murdered. How will you avenge them? We, the Soviet Jews – we are doing our duty, we shall come to the day of trial as a fighting people and we shall ask you what you have done to help us?

In its appeals to the Western Jews to provide help to the Red Army and Soviet people in their fight against the Nazis, the JAC was permitted to say that Soviet Jews were an integral part of world Jewry and to refer to the solidarity and brotherhood of the Jews across the globe. This went against Lenin's and Stalin's theory that there could be no solidarity between the Jews living in different countries as an ethnic or religious group and that unity and solidarity could only be between proletarians of all nations. In 1943 Stalin sent Mikhoels and Fefer to USA, Canada, Mexico and Great Britain. Western Jewish organizations considered their visit a first step towards building links between Soviet Jews and world Jewry which had practically stopped during Stalin's reign. Their leaders, including those in Great Britain, greeted Mikhoels and Fefer with great enthusiasm and often expressed the hope that after the war Soviet Jews would have religious freedom and become an integral part of world Jewry.

The *Jewish Standard,* in its issue published on 17 September 1943, wrote:

> The Jews of this country will extend a welcome to Mikhoels and Fefer, and will mark the occasion by impressing them with the great sense of satisfaction and gratitude felt at this first contact between the Jews of Britain and the Soviet Jews. We shall have among us our brothers – Jews with whom we will be able to exchange thoughts and views in the hope that it will bring us back into permanent association with the lost limb of the House of Israel.

The *Russian Jews in the War* also contains a statement by Dr S. Brodetsky, the then President of the Board of Deputies of British Jews (and future President of the Hebrew University in Jerusalem),

> I hope this struggle with Nazism will bring freedom also to the Jews in every country and an equal status for the Jewish people among the nations of the World. I would urge the Jews to give liberally to the Jewish Fund for Soviet Russia because it is doing something for the great Russian people which is bravely helping to liberate the World, to create a World in which all people, and the Jewish people among them will be free and able to live their own life.

The Chief Rabbi Hertz also appealed to all British Jews: 'Russia is fighting our fight, and the Battle of Britain is being continued in Russia . . . As citizens, the Jews of this country are like all others doing their share to help Russia by contributing to Mrs Churchill's Fund. But as Jews, should we not do something over and above our contribution as citizens?'

As can be seen from the content of the booklet, Mikhoels and Fefer were allowed to meet Western Zionist leaders. These meeting were unique occasions, because, during the previous 25 years, the Soviet authorities tried to eradicate all traces of Zionism – anyone in the USSR who tried to spread Zionist ideas was considered an enemy of the state, sent to a labour camp or even executed.

Chaim Weizmann, the Zionist leader and the future first President of Israel, made the following statement at a press conference in London:

For the first time after 25 years it was my great privilege and a moving hour for me to meet the delegation which came over from Moscow to visit the American Jewish community. This delegation will also come here. It consists of a famous actor, the head of the Yiddish theatre in Moscow and a distinguished poet. I had a long conversation – three hours, in fact – and we covered a fair amount of ground and I get a picture of what the Russian Jewish community is like. I believe they are interested in Zionism, but at any rate they are not opposed to it; they were very discreet and made no statement, but it was extremely interesting for one to listen to them, to hear about the cultural life of the Jewish community. I was greatly interested to meet S. Mikhoels and I. Fefer in New York and look forward to meeting them again on their arrival in this country.

The booklet also includes an excerpt from an article in *Jewish Labour* (September 1943) by S. Levenberg, Editor of the *Zionist Review,* head of the Jewish Agency, UK, member of the World Zionist Action Committee and the Chairman of Israel Committee of the Board of Deputies:

There is no logical reason why there should be a conflict between the World Jewry and the Soviet Union and why Russia should not be among the foremost supporters of the Jewish National home in Palestine. A policy of understanding is in the interest of the Jewish people in the USSR. There can be no doubt that the responsible Jewish leadership and the Zionist Socialist Movement, in particular, are prepared to work towards that end.

There is also an excerpt from an editorial in the *Zionist Review:*

It is no exaggeration to say that the fate of the Jewish National Home may be decided in the course of the present gigantic battles in the Soviet Union. We hope there is no Jew who does not realise this fact. Together with their fellow citizens Jews in the free countries must do everything in their power to help the Soviet people.

After the revolution, the Soviet authorities tried to suppress all religion, including Judaism. Most synagogues were closed down, and many rabbis were arrested. The situation changed somewhat during the Second World War, when permission was given to open new synagogues and the authorities turned a blind eye to Jews participating in religious services.

The JAC was allowed, therefore, to send to the West some material which created an impression of religious freedom in the USSR. Two such documents are included in the booklet. One is an appeal from the congregation of a synagogue:

> Brother Jews of Great Britain, USA and of other countries. We, the Jews, assembled in our synagogue, facing the Torah and our prayer books in our hands, appeal to you, brother Jews. All who believe in God must join in this self-sacrificing struggle against Fascism, with weapons in their hands, to defend their religion and to protect mankind from this savage foe. Brothers Jews do your duty. Help the great heroic Red Army. Victory is near. Let us hasten its coming!

A moving letter also appeared in *The Russian Jews in the War* to show that there were still traditional religious Jews living in the Soviet Union (the JAC presents it as a typical example of a large number of similar letters in its possession). Hirsch Smilanski, aged 65, writes to his son Chaim, a lieutenant in the Soviet Air Force stationed on the Stalingrad front:

> There was not enough room in our synagogue during the celebration of Rosh Hashana and Yom Kippur. With broken hearts and with eyes filled with tears we prayed to God that He should send a swift downfall upon this man of blood, Hitler, and his whole gang. Every day we pray for the victory of the Red Army and for the survival of our people. We hope that God will hear our prayers. I want you to know, my dear son, that a prayer is also not lost in the war.

Mikhoels, in his message to the Jews of Great Britain and the USA, included the following words – words which were, to put it mildly, very unusual for a Soviet public figure,

> In their prayers on Yom Kippur our forefathers said, 'May our prayers rise from eventide; may our cry come before You at the dawn; let our redemption come' This is the prayer that has been born in the blood of the Jewish people through the suffering of the Jewish mothers and wives, through the pain and anguish of Jewish sisters.

The results of the JAC mission

The four-month trip to Western countries by Mikhoels and Fefer brought spectacular results. In the USA, Mikhoels and Fefer had numerous meetings with politicians, businessmen, writers and actors. As a result of these meetings, committees of help to the Soviet people and the Red Army were established, money, jewellery, clothing, medicines were shipped to the Soviet Union. The USA Committee for Aid to Russia collected $16 million. A million complete sets of clothing and a hundred thousand watches for the soldiers of the Red Army were gathered in Chicago alone. The American Joint Distribution Committee allocated several million dollars to help the Soviet people evacuated from the territories occupied by the German troops. A million dollars was collected in Mexico.

Mrs Churchill's 'Aid to Russia' provided 15 million dollars. The Soviet Jewish doctors sent an appeal to the Jews of Great Britain signed on their behalf by Dr B.Shimeliovich, head of the main Moscow hospital, and Professor M. Averbach, a world-leading ophthalmologist and a member of the Soviet Academy of Sciences, 'We call upon you, the Jewish doctors of Great Britain to help equip the Red Army, to provide them with medical aid, to help them to drive out the enemy from Soviet territory and to help us to save the Jewish people from extermination.'

In response to this appeal, the Jewish Fund decided to collect £50,000 to provide the Red Army with 25 mobile X-ray units. The Soviet Union's Ambassador to the United Kingdom, M. Maisky, sent the following message to the Jewish Fund for Soviet Russia:

'Will you please convey my sincere thanks to all those who have organized this effort in aid of the Jewish Fund for Soviet Russia and to all those who have supported their efforts. The contribution you are making in aid of my country is warmly appreciated and I send you every good wish for success.'

The compilers of *The Russian Jews in the War* particularly emphasized the help provided by the Jews living in Palestine to the Soviet war efforts:

> The Jews of Palestine were the first to respond to the call of the Jewish Anti-Fascist Committee of the USSR. We read in the *Pravda* newspaper that the representatives of the Palestine Victory League have arrived in Teheran and have brought with them as a contribution for the Red Army from the Jews of Palestine two ambulances and one field hospital fully equipped for the Front. The representatives of the Palestine Victory League report that they were stopped on their way by the throngs of people, workers and farmers, who had contributed towards buying these ambulances and who asked that their greetings should be conveyed to the Red Army fighters.

A cheque for £10,000 was presented to the Soviet Ambassador to the UK, M. Maisky, at the Soviet Embassy in London. This money had been collected by the General Federation of Jewish Labour (Histadrut).

The political results of the trip by Mikhoels and Fefer were no less significant. For example, millions of Americans demanded the opening of a second front in Europe.

The JAC played an important role during the war in highlighting the heroism of the Jewish people fighting the Nazis in the ranks of the Red Army and their achievements in providing the Army with necessary armaments in the plants and factories in unoccupied territories. At the same time, the JAC collected material about the extermination of the Jewish population by the Nazis in the occupied area of the USSR (the booklet contains much material on this topic). Gradually, in the absence of other organizations representing Soviet Jews, the JAC became the body which Soviet Jews considered as their representative – where they sent their grievances, complaints and suggestions. Stalin did not like this because he was afraid of the rise of the Jewish nationalism. He had created the JAC for one purpose only – to collect money for the war efforts.

The demise of the JAC

Immediately after the war Stalin unleashed his antisemitic policy. The JAC and its leaders, who hoped to continue their activities, were doomed. The first victim was the Chairman of the JAC, Solomon Mikhoels. It was announced in January 1948 that he had died in a car accident, but the Jews suspected that he had been killed on Stalin's orders. Later, when Svetlana Allilueva, Stalin's daughter, escaped to the West, she corroborated this in her book *"Only One Year"* (1969).

In the autumn of 1948, the newly appointed Ambassador, Golda Meir, and other members of the Israel embassy in Moscow went to the synagogue to attend the Jewish New Year service. Fifty thousand Jews greeted them outside the building and later formed a procession to accompany them part of the way back to the embassy It was a spontaneous demonstration of a Jewish attachment to Israel which Stalin considered dangerous and treacherous. He decided to put an end to such national aspirations and the remnants of Jewish culture. On 20 November 1948 the JAC was disbanded. The Yiddish newspaper *Einikait*, published by the JAC, which had always taken a pro-Israeli line, was closed down on the same day; its editors and many journalists were arrested. The only Yiddish publishing house *Der Emes* was also shut down; its director, editor-in-chief, and many rank-and-file employees were arrested. The famous Yiddish theatre in Moscow and all the other Yiddish theatres in other cities across the Soviet Union were closed down. And in 1949 many leading members of the JAC were arrested, among them writers and poets (I. Fefer, P. Markish, D. Bergelson, D. Gofshtein, L. Kvitko), the great Yiddish actor V. Zuskin, the head of the main Moscow hospital, B. Shimeliovich, and a well-known physiologist, L. Shtern, member of the Soviet Academy of Sciences. Many Jews (scholars, engineers, writers, singers and others) were later arrested under the charge of Jewish bourgeois nationalism and espionage. Synagogues were closed across the Soviet Union, rabbis and lay leaders of Jewish communities arrested. After a closed trial in Moscow during 11-18 July 1952, 13 members of the JAC (including I. Fefer) were condemned to death; on 12 August 1952 they were executed; the other members were sent to labour camps.

This year the Jewish world will commemorate the fifty-fifth anniversary of this tragic event. At the time of the 'Doctors' plot' in 1953, Mikhoels was posthumously accused of being 'an agent of the World Zionist organization 'Joint'. This was how Stalin rewarded Mikhoels and Feffer for their massive campaign in the West in support of the Soviet war efforts.

The aftermath

I vividly remember how in our flat in Leningrad (as, probably, in every other Jewish home in the Soviet Union) in the years 1949-53 we would burn any books, newspapers and any other documents in which Mikhoels, Fefer and other arrested members of the JAC were mentioned because it was dangerous to keep them. If by some miracle the booklet *The Russian Jews in the War* had been found in the house of a Soviet Jew, he or she would immediately have been arrested and, at best, sent to a labour camp for many years.

As I have described above, the visit to the West of Mikhoels and Fefer created many hopes for the revival of Soviet Jewry. These hopes were brutally crushed by Stalin. Indeed the closure of Jewish institutions, the execution and arrest of prominent Jewish leaders in many different fields, amounted to the total destruction of Jewish culture in the Soviet Union. In 1943, in his appeal to British Jews published in the booklet, Chief Rabbi Hertz said: 'Let us remember that if we do our full duty we not only help to smash Hitlerism but bring back Russian Jewry to the fold of Israel.'

The hopes of Rabbi Hertz were to be fulfilled, alas, only after the collapse of the Soviet Union, almost fifty years later.

8

Jews who fought alongside the Germans

Originally published in the Jewish Quarterly,
vol. 53, issue 2, 2006, pp 25-26

This is the extraordinary story of the Finnish Jewish soldiers who fought alongside the Germans in the Second World War.

Despite 60 years' intensive research and thousands of publications, certain aspects of the Second World War are still little known or remain to be discovered. It is only now, that it has become possible to reconstruct the full story of Finland's participation in the war. Consider the incredible paradox. Finland fought on the side of Germany (although it always refused to call itself an ally and insisted that it was only a co-belligerent). Yet it refused to deport, persecute or even discriminate against its Jewish population. And the country even behaved humanely towards Jewish prisoners of war. Even stranger, Jewish soldiers initially fought in the Finnish ranks as equals, which inevitably, helped the Germans achieve some of their war aims. Later in the war, they had an opportunity to take part in the fight against the Germans.

Before 1809, when Finland became part of the Russian Empire, there was no Jewish population in Finland at all. In 1827 Tsar Nicholas I issued an edict requiring Jewish boys from the age of 12 – who became known as Cantonists – to undertake 25 years of compulsory military service. The main aim of this edict, abolished only in 1856, was to assimilate and eventually convert the Jews to Christianity. Yet the soldiers who completed their military service were allowed to live anywhere in the Russian Empire, and many remained in the last place where they had been stationed. Hence some Jewish soldiers settled in Finland and, since there were no Jewish brides there, asked matchmakers from the Pale of Settlement to help them find wives. In the absence of railways, unmarried girls and widows were transported there by horse-driven carts (in fact, when the former Cantonists were asked, 'How did you meet your wife?', they would reply, 'I got her from a cart.'). This was the beginning of the Finnish Jewish continuity. After the 1917 Revolution some more Jews emigrated from Russia and settled in Finland, increasing their number to 2,000. (Finland became independent in 1918.) A further influx arrived after 1938, when the leaders of the Finnish Jewish community asked the government to provide entry visas for Austrian Jews – whom they offered to provide for without requiring any public funds. Altogether, 300 Jewish refugees from Austria, Germany and Czechoslovakia came to Finland.

In December 1939, the Soviet Union started a war with Finland, in order to gain territory. In the initial stages of the conflict (known in Finland as the Winter War) the Finnish army under Marshal Mannerheim successfully repelled the numerically superior Red Army. Then, in February 1940, Soviet troops managed to break the main defensive line (the so-called Mannerheim Line), although they continued to suffer heavy losses due to fierce resistance. The peace treaty of March 1940 forced Finland to cede parts of its territory.

From the Jewish point of view, this war was highly significant. It was the first time since the First World War that Jewish soldiers had fought on both sides of a front line. Many Jews served with distinction in the Finnish army, where they were treated as equals; 15 were killed in battle. But many Jews also fought in the ranks of the Red Army. Lieutenant Leonid Buber, for example, was awarded the highest honour of Hero of the Soviet Union for his part in breaking the Mannerheim Line. In charge of a rifle company, he was wounded three times but did not leave the battlefield. He was later appointed a member of the Jewish Anti-Fascist Committee and was one of the few who miraculously survived after most were exterminated on Stalin's orders in 1952.

In 1940 two Scandinavian countries – Denmark and Norway – were occupied by the Germans. Finland faced a stark choice: also being occupied or becoming another Soviet Republic like Latvia, Estonia and Lithuania. Occupation was a very real danger since the German army could easily enter Finland from Norway, with a view to using its long frontier as a springboard for attacking the Soviet Union. Its substantial nickel deposits were also needed for military purposes. In the event, the Finnish government chose to join forces with Germany in the hope of regaining the territory it had lost in the Winter War and so declared war on the Soviet Union on 25 June 1941, three days after Germany attacked the USSR. (This was the start of what is known in Finland as the Continuation War).

The German army was permitted to deploy in Lapland, in the north of the country, so to attack the Soviet Union from there. All this led Great Britain to declare war on Finland. By August 1941 the Finnish troops under the command of Marshal Mannerheim had managed to regain the lost territories and almost reached the pre-Winter War border, securing positions on the shores of Lake Ladoga, on the Karelian Isthmus and on the Svir river. It was here the front stabilized until the summer of 1944 – something which allowed Finnish troops to play a crucial role in the further course of fighting between the Germans and Russians.

Despite the presence of German troops in Finland and the German command and Gestapo in Helsinki, Finland rejected Hitler's demands to introduce anti-Jewish laws. Neither in Finland, nor in the parts of the USSR occupied by Finland, were Jews persecuted. Hitler twice came to Finland and tried in vain to persuade the Finnish authorities to deport the Jewish population. Only in a single case, near the start of the war, did the head of the Finnish police agree to extradite eight Jews without Finnish citizenship, seven of whom were immediately murdered. When the Finnish media reported on this, a huge scandal broke out and ministers resigned in protest. (In spring 1944, 160 Jewish refugees who did not have Finnish citizenship were transported to neutral Sweden to save their lives – on the orders of Marshal Mannerheim, commander of the Finnish army).

During the war, the lives of the Finnish Jews continued as before: synagogues and communal installations functioned, and a Jewish newspaper was published. Three hundred Jewish officers and soldiers served in the Finnish army during the Continuation War (eight were killed in battle). Yet they faced an agonizing dilemma. Those who took part in the Winter War knew that they were fighting against an aggressor. Now Jewish soldiers understood that, by serving in an army fighting the USSR, they were also helping Hitler. Throughout the Continuation War, they collaborated with the Germans. Some who were fluent in German served in the Intelligence Service and so, through the constant liaison with German Intelligence, acquired information about the extermination of European Jewry. On the other hand, Jewish soldiers remembered the words of Marshal Mannerheim when Hitler tried to persuade Finnish leaders to deport the Jews to concentration camps, 'While Jews serve in my army I will not allow their deportation.' By serving in the Finnish army Jewish soldiers hoped to prevent the community from being persecuted. The maintenance of Jewish religious tradition was of paramount importance to soldiers fighting on the Finnish-Soviet front. A field synagogue was established a mere two kilometres from the German troops. This was the only field synagogue on the German side of the 2,000-mile front line, which in 1942 stretched all the way from the North Cape in Norway to El Alamein in Egypt. The Finnish High Command granted leave to Jewish soldiers on

Saturdays and Jewish holidays. Worshippers came to pray from near and far, some on skis, some on horseback, most on foot. The Germans were astonished and frustrated to see Jewish soldiers holding religious services in an army tent. It is also interesting to note that the most popular Finnish singer, the 'soldier's sweetheart' (a Finnish Vera Lynn), was Jewish. Yet she entertained only Finnish soldiers and refused to do the same for the Germans.

Three Jews serving in the Finnish army were awarded Iron Crosses by the German command for their bravery (see Hannu Rautkallio, 'Cast into the Lion's Den', Journal of Contemporary History Vol 29, 1994). Major Leo Skurnik was a descendant of one of the oldest Cantonist Jewish families. He served as a doctor, organized the evacuation of a German field hospital and thereby saved the lives of more than 600 German officers and soldiers. He refused to accept the decoration on the grounds of being a Jew. Captain Solomon Klass saved a German company that had been surrounded by Soviet forces. Two days later, German officers came to offer him the Iron Cross. He refused to stand up and told them contemptuously that he was Jewish and did not want their medal. The officers repeated their 'Heil Hitler' salute and left. A third Jew, a nurse, also refused the Iron Cross.

Information about Soviet Jewish prisoners of war captured by Finnish troops only became available recently. Some very interesting reminiscences by one such prisoner, Lazar Raskin, appeared in a special issue of the Jewish journal Lechaim (published in Russian, in Moscow) devoted to the sixtieth anniversary of victory in Europe in May 2005. Raskin served as a soldier in the Red Army and, after being wounded, was taken prisoner by Finnish soldiers and sent to hospital. Later, along with more than a hundred other Soviet Jewish prisoners, he was transferred to a special camp where the conditions were marginally better than in other prisoner-of-war camps. They were assigned to a factory producing fertilizers. Raskin spent two and a half years there, and as he later recalled:

> In spring 1943 we were informed that several Finnish Jews were coming to our camp. We were extremely surprised because we did not think that there were Jews in Finland and that they were free to come and go. Three elderly men came and introduced themselves as representatives of the Helsinki Jewish community. They brought boxes with matzot and told us that Passover was imminent. They also brought books. including stories by Sholem Aleichem and I. L Peretz and 'The History of the Jews' by the famous historian S. Dubnov (all in Yiddish). In the evening after work, we spent time

with our visitors. We felt at ease with them and had a friendly chat in Yiddish. Just the fact that we saw Jews before us, safe and prosperous, made it a festive occasion. We knew what the Nazis were doing to the European Jewry. The visitors told us that the Finnish authorities, despite the demands of the Germans, not only did not persecute the Jews but even defended their interests. Later we sang Jewish songs together. Surprisingly, the Finnish Jews knew the same songs as we did. The prisoners also realized that the representatives of the Jewish community had spoken to the manager of the factory. After their visit the food we were given got better and the regime less strict. The visit left a pleasant impression, and we remembered it for a long rime. The most precious presents were the books. Because very few people could read Yiddish, I read aloud the stories of Sholem Aleichem and everybody laughed. I studied the *History of the Jews* very thoroughly and later gave several lectures on this on the line. Everybody listened very attentively because for most of us the history of our people was unknown.

After the peace treaty between the Soviet Union and Finland was signed in 1944, the Soviet prisoners of war were sent back to the USSR. It is interesting that Lazar Raskin, like most of his fellow prisoners, was not allowed to go home to his family but sent to work in the coal mines on Stalin's orders. He was released only after Stalin's death in 1953. It is obvious that the policy of the Finnish authorities towards the Jews was in striking contrast to the situation not only in Germany, but also in the Allied countries, including the occupied countries such as France, where the Vichy government actively helped to round up the Jews.

One of the main reasons for this was the personality of the great Finnish leader Carl Gustav Mannerheim (1867-1951). He was a general of the Imperial Russian Army, served as a Garde du Chevalier officer to the Tsarina and accompanied Tsar Nicholas I and the Tsarina during their coronation in Moscow in 1896. He was also a scientist and explorer of Asia and the Far East. After the Russian Revolution in 1917 he became a leader of the Finnish army that suppressed a rebellion by Bolshevik forces. It was as a result of this that Finland became an independent state. During the period from 1927 to 1939 he built the system of fortifications along the border with the USSR known as 'the Mannerheim Line' – which the Soviet Union, in 1939, paid a heavy price in breaking through. Stalin long remembered the lesson he had been taught by Mannerheim: fierce Finnish resistance saved the country from becoming a Soviet Republic.

Mannerheim's war aims were quite different from those of the Germans he fought alongside. He merely wanted to recover Finnish territory lost in the Winter War and to preserve the country's independence. He had no desire to destroy the USSR. because, as he once put it, 'Russia will always be our neighbour.' And he never pursued Hitler's racial policies. Indeed, he helped ensure that Finnish Jews had equal rights with the Christian majority.

One of the decisive battles of the Second World War was the siege of Leningrad. At the end of August 1941, the city was completely surrounded by German and Finnish troops, with the latter holding positions almost all around Lake Ladoga. The Russians controlled only part of its south-eastern shore. Because food stocks were destroyed by German bombers, a million inhabitants of Leningrad died of hunger and cold during the unusually harsh winter of 1941-2. The only way in and out of the city was over Lake Ladoga. Hence, under the most difficult conditions, a road – known as *'the road of life'* – was built from Leningrad to the unoccupied Soviet territory via the frozen lake. It was along this road that hundreds of thousands of children, the sick and the wounded were evacuated from Leningrad during 1941-2 and food, armaments and ammunition brought into the city. If it had not been for this road, Leningrad would never have been able to survive and fight on against the Germans. Yet the Finnish troops positioned around the lake could easily have destroyed *'the road of life'*. Hitler proclaimed at the beginning of the war that he would raze Leningrad to the ground. This did not happen purely because Mannerheim did not want it to happen, and so he refused to order his troops to attack *'the road of life'*. If Finland had not occupied the Karelian Isthmus and the shores of Lake Ladoga, the Germans would have been there – and Leningrad would have been destroyed. Mannerheim's decision saved this great city and the 150,000 Jews (including my father, Shmuel Shapiro) who lived and worked there during the siege.

Equally significant were the two naval ports that had not frozen over, Murmansk and Archangelsk, in the north of the USSR. Since Britain and the USA organized Arctic convoys to deliver armaments, ammunition, vehicles and food, the Germans often asked Mannerheim to bomb the railways to the ports and to cut off all communications with the North. At the beginning of 1943, Hitler came to Finland for a day to congratulate Mannerheim on his 75th birthday. According to Soviet historians, Mannerheim assured Hitler that the Finnish army would undertake these operations after the fall of Leningrad. Yet this was just a ruse to gain time – he did not want Hitler to defeat the Soviet Union.

In August 1944 Mannerheim was elected President of Finland and initiated peace negotiations with the USSR. The Armistice Agreement was signed in September 1944. According to this agreement Finland started military actions against German troops deployed in Lapland – an action in which some Finnish Jewish soldiers also took part. On 6 December (Independence Day) 1944 President Mannerheim visited the Helsinki synagogue, took part in a commemorative service for the Jewish soldiers who had died in the Winter and Continuation Wars and presented the Jewish community with a medal. It was because of Mannerheim that Finland remained an independent state, unlike the many East European countries which became satellites of the Soviet Union. Finnish Jews continued to have every opportunity to live as Jews in a vibrant community or to emigrate to Israel. Twenty-seven Jews with battle experience went there in 1948 to take part in the War of Independence.

In 2005 an exhibition dedicated to Marshal Mannerheim was held at the Hermitage Museum in St Petersburg, and Finnish historians had an opportunity to show for the first time Mannerheim's role in saving Leningrad. It is here, perhaps, that the Finnish Jewish soldiers who took part in the Second World War on the German side can take consolation. By fighting alongside the Germans, paradoxically, they helped to save not only the Finnish Jewish community but also the great city of Leningrad and its Jewish community.

9

The 'Doctors Plot' and the death of Stalin

Originally published in the Jewish Quarterly,
vol. 50, issue 1, 2003, pp 56-58

The first four months of 1953 – from 13 January to 6 April – marked a turning point in the life of Soviet Jews. Most Soviet Jews who were alive at the time, I am sure, still remember what we were doing when we heard the shocking announcement of the arrest of the Jewish 'doctor-murderers'.

I will certainly never forget that day. I was living in Leningrad and on my way to school that morning as usual. It was a beautiful day. Fresh snow, which had fallen at night, sparkled. The sky was cloudless and blue. I was thinking that after school I would be going skiing in the park. Suddenly I noticed an unusually large crowd assembled near a newspaper stand where the daily issue of *Pravda* was always displayed. I heard Jewish surnames spoken, accompanied by the words 'doctors' and 'murderers'. I immediately understood that something terrible had happened. When I came home after school, I saw that my mother was very upset and her eyes red from crying. In front of her she had a copy of *Pravda* with the announcement about the arrest of the Jewish doctors. At the time, of course, I could not appreciate the full significance and enormity of this event. It was not until later, listening to the reminiscences of my parents and relatives and reading about this period that I came to understand what had happened in the Soviet Union in early 1953. This brief account is based on my own and my relatives' recollections, as well as on the new materials recently discovered in Soviet archives and published in G. Kostyrchenko's *'Secret Policy of Stalin'* (2001).

The antisemitic policies of the Soviet government intensified after the Second World War and 1948-53 proved the worst years for the Soviet Jews. Solomon Michoels, a well-known actor and *de facto* leader of the Soviet Jews, was killed on 13 January 1948 – on the personal orders of Stalin. In

November 1948 the Jewish Anti-Fascist Committee was disbanded. Its members were arrested and accused of 'close connections with Jewish nationalist organizations in the USA, and of sending those organizations secret facts about Soviet economics and slanderous information about the situation of Jews in the USSR.' They were also accused of trying to settle Jews in Crimea to organize a Jewish republic there, which the USA would use as springboard for an attack on the USSR. All the defendants (except one woman) were condemned to death and executed on 12 August 1952.

An openly malicious antisemitic campaign began with an article in *Pravda* in January 1949. The campaign was officially directed against so-called 'cosmopolitans', but everybody had understood that 'cosmopolitans' meant 'Jews'. Purges began everywhere in the country. They affected Jews working in economics, science, medicine and the arts. Many Jewish specialists were dismissed, some were arrested and several executed. The anti-Jewish campaign reached its climax with 'The Doctors' Plot'. On 13 January 1953, all the newspapers in the USSR published the following:

> *Announcement of TASS (Telegraph Agency of the Soviet Union): Arrest of the group of the doctor-saboteurs,* A terrorist group of doctors was discovered recently by State Security. Their aim was to shorten the life of active statesmen of the Soviet Union by providing deliberately harmful treatment ... It was established that all these doctor-murderers. who became the monsters of mankind, were hired agents of the foreign Intelligence Services. Most of the members of this terrorist group (Vovsi, Feldman, Etinger, Grinshtein and others) were connected with the International Jewish bourgeois-nationalist organization 'Joint', set up by American Intelligence supposedly to provide financial help to the Jews in other countries. In fact, this organization, under the guidance of America Intelligence, carried out wide-ranging espionage, terrorist and other subversive activities in several countries including the Soviet Union.

This announcement was approved prior to publication by the Presidium of the Central Committee of the Communist Party of the Soviet Union. Stalin had sanctioned the torture of the arrested doctors to extract their confessions, and the doctors were brutally beaten during interrogation. Of the 37 Moscow doctors arrested twenty-eight were Jewish.

Immediately after the publication of the above announcement the media began an antisemitic campaign. The name of Lydia Timashuk, an ordinary doctor in the Kremlin hospital, suddenly acquired great prominence. At the instigation of State Security she gave 'evidence' that famous doctors hastened the death of two members of the Politburo through deliberate wrong treatment. On 21 January (the anniversary of Lenin's death), *Pravda* published the following decree:

For help given to the government in unmasking the doctor-killers Dr Lydia Timashuk is awarded 'The order of Lenin' (the highest Soviet decoration).

The media proclaimed her a national heroine and praised her 'patriotic deed'. One of the most popular journals published an article called 'The Poisoners' about the arrested doctors, which contained the following paragraph: "This scum of society ... used their own position as doctors for committing murders. They carried out orders given by their masters to eliminate Soviet leaders".

State Security fabricated cases against doctors, many of whom were arrested. A typical case took place in a town in Belorussia, where a group of young doctors sent a denunciation to the State Security, accusing the Jewish doctors of conducting fatal experiments on Belorussian patients, and only treating properly their Jewish patients. Throughout the entire country patients refused treatment from Jewish doctors, and the latter were afraid to go to work. In every issue of all Soviet newspapers, articles were published about illegal activities committed by Jews such as embezzlement, private commerce and underground production of consumer goods. Everywhere Jews were vilified, and no one felt immune from persecution.

After the TASS announcement of 'The Doctors' Plot' meetings were held where speakers demanded a tougher policy towards Jews; people sent letters to Stalin asking him to deport all Jews from the European part of the USSR. There were real fears of a new wave of terror. There were rumours that lists of Jews had already been drawn up, that Stalin had given orders for several hundred special trains to be brought to Moscow (and other large cities) in order to transport Jews to the Far East. People were openly saying that barracks to accommodate the deported Jews had already been built. There were even rumours that children would be taken away from their parents and sent to orphanages, rumours that the arrested doctors would be publicly executed. Well-disposed gentiles often advised their Jewish friends to prepare an overnight bag for every member of the family, complete with warm clothes and documents.

I, myself, witnessed such a warning. My father, a World War Two veteran, had a gentile friend from his army days who had become a high-ranking Party official. One Sunday morning, at the end of January, he unexpectedly dropped in on us and invited me to go skating with his daughter on the open-air rink in the nearby park. My father was to accompany us. I found out later that, while his daughter and I were skating, he told my father about the rumours among local officials of the impending deportation of all the Jews and strongly advised us to be prepared. The next day my mother bought bags for the whole family, packed them and put them under our beds. We were ready! People who had relatives abroad felt especially vulnerable because they were afraid that they would be accused of spying for foreign countries. They stopped all correspondence with even their closest relatives and burned all letters and photographs. Stalin ordered a letter to *Pravda* to be prepared, which had to be signed by more than 50 famous scientists, actors, writers, servicemen, military aircraft designers and doctors, as well as selected workers and collective farmers. The letter was to acknowledge the common guilt of all Soviet Jews for 'The Doctors' Plot' and to propose that, in atonement for this crime, they should go into voluntary exile in the Soviet Far East. Very few people refused to sign, although the well-known writer, Ilya Ehrenburg, wrote a letter to Stalin, suggesting that he would damage Soviet prestige amongst Communist Parties abroad. For this or other reasons, the letter was never published. Yet in his book '*People, Years, Life*' Ehrenburg wrote that 'Stalin did not have time to do what he wanted.'

Some Russian historians deny that deportation of the Soviet Jews was imminent. This view is based on the fact that no documents relating to the deportation have yet been found in the Russian archives. Other historians, basing their arguments on circumstantial evidence, claim that all the relevant documents were destroyed after Stalin's death. Yet they quote, for example, from '*How It Was*' (1999), the memoirs of Anastas Mikoyan, one of Stalin 's henchmen: 'The voluntary-compulsory expulsion of Jews from Moscow was prepared. The death of Stalin prevented the execution of this plan.' Whatever the eventual outcome of these debates, for every Jew who lived in the Soviet Union 50 years ago the threat of deportation seemed real – and life became almost unbearable. Everybody understood that only Stalin's death could improve the situation for the Jews, but most of them did not think it would happen soon. In 1953 Stalin was only 73, and many believed that he would live to an age of a hundred, like so many of his Georgian countrymen.

Thirty-five years after the October Revolution there were only a handful of religious Jews in the Soviet Union. They prayed that the festival of Purim, which in 1953 fell on 1 March, would bring deliverance to the Jews. And it so happened that exactly on that day Stalin had a cerebral haemorrhage: he died three days later. Less than a month after Stalin's death on 4 April 1953, the following announcement in all the newspapers came like a bombshell:

> *Announcement of the USSR Ministry of Internal Affairs* – The USSR Ministry of Internal Affairs has carried out a thorough examination of all the materials of the preliminary investigation and other facts relevant to the case of the group of the doctors accused of sabotage, espionage and terrorist acts against the leaders of the Soviet Union. After this examination it has been established that the doctors involved in this case were arrested by the Ministry of State Security wrongly, without any lawful grounds. The examination has proved that accusations brought against all of them were false and the data on which the investigators based their accusations were unfounded. It has been established that testimonies of the arrested, allegedly confirming the accusations brought against them, were obtained by the investigators of the Ministry of State Security using methods of investigation inadmissible and strictly forbidden by the Soviet laws.

All the arrested doctors were released on 3 and 4 April. They were ordered 'to forget everything' and not to tell anyone what had happened to them. On the same day, the Presidium of the Supreme Soviet revoked its decree of 21 January decorating Dr L Timashuk and stated that 'the decoration was based on incorrect information'. For Soviet Jews these events were a cause for celebration. Now cleared of the slanderous stigma of 'murderers', they openly congratulated each other, even in the street or at work. I vividly remember a celebration, spontaneously organized in our flat, with many relatives and friends attending. This was not the end of our surprises. On 6 April, the editorial in *Pravda* called the doctors 'The most honest and respected citizens of our State'. Solomon Michoels was praised as 'the most honourable public figure, the People's Artist of the USSR who was slandered by people "without conscience". For everybody in the Soviet Union these announcements came as a watershed.

The end of 'The Doctors' Plot' symbolized the start of a new era which was named *'The Thaw'* after a famous book by Ilya Ehrenburg. For former Soviet Jews who lived through those times and still celebrate Purim, it has become a festival not only commemorating the deliverance of the Jews from the wicked Haman but also the deliverance from Stalin in 1953.

The plate 9.1 shows the 'Unmasked doctor-murderer': a typical cartoon from a popular Soviet magazine printed at the time of 'The Doctors' Plot'.

It was understood by everybody then. The hand grabbing the 'doctor-murderer' represents the Soviet State Security. The mask shows the typical benevolent medical professor depicted in Russian folk art. It covers up the real face of a murderous gangster in dark glasses. The coins falling from the doctor's pockets represent the money he supposedly received for his crimes.

10

Growing up Jewish in Leningrad

Originally published in Jewish Renaissance,
vol. 10, issue 2, 2011, pp 20-21

I was born before WWII in a Jewish religious family in Leningrad. My parents, Shmuel and Sheindl Shapiro, came to Leningrad from Slavuta in Ukraine. Most of the Jewish population of Leningrad (more than 180,000 before the war) came from different parts of the former Pale of Settlement of the Russian Empire.

After the Germans attacked the USSR on 22 June 1941, our family was evacuated to the Urals. My father, who joined the Soviet Army, was wounded at the Leningrad front and sent to a hospital in the city for treatment. Many factories that produced civilian goods before the War became part of the military industrial effort. When my father recovered, he was appointed the director of such a factory where he had worked before the War. It started to produce mortars that went straight from the factory gates to the Front. My father lived in Leningrad during the whole 900 days of its siege. In 1944 we returned to Leningrad, were reunited with my father and started to rebuild our life. My parents were deeply religious and maintained the Jewish way of life in spite of tremendous difficulties and even danger.

The majority of the Jewish population in Leningrad was gradually assimilated, never set foot in a synagogue and was unfamiliar with the Jewish religion and traditions. Due to the antisemitic and anti-religious state policy it was almost impossible to receive any form of Jewish education or to have the facilities necessary to maintain a Jewish way of life. There were probably not more than 500 families which, like ours, kept the Jewish faith and customs. My parents regularly prayed in the synagogue, especially on Jewish holidays. I was taught Hebrew and basic Judaism by a clandestine rebbe (teacher). I had Jewish and non-Jewish friends and kept our observance secret from all. I accepted this as a normal way of life. I went to synagogue with my parents as a child but was afraid to go once I had started university and later when I was working. To buy kosher meat my mother had to go at 6am to one of the Leningrad markets and stand in a queue for several hours, because kosher meat was sold only once a week and the supply was very small. It was difficult to buy matzot for Passover because only a small amount was baked. One had to be very careful in order not to be denounced to the authorities as being observant. For example, it was dangerous to openly put mezuzahs on the doors. My father placed all mezuzahs in our flat within the wooden door architraves, for them not to be openly seen.

To show how dangerous it was to be religious during Stalin's time I can cite, as an example, the life of a close friend of our family. He was a deeply religious Jew who studied in a yeshiva before the revolution. He dedicated his life to the service of his fellow Jews. He was a member of the managing board of the Great Choral synagogue, organised the production of matzot for Passover and supplied them to the members of his community. He managed to bring etrogim from Moscow for Succot. In 1950 he was summoned for interrogation to the Leningrad office of the State Security who demanded that he name his 'accomplices'. He refused and died on the street from a heart attack. He was only 54 years old.

My husband and I were married in 1962. For security reasons our chuppah took place in Kharkov, where his uncle lived. It was conducted in a private flat and only our parents, relatives and a very small number of close friends, who came from several cities of the USSR, were present at the wedding. Our ketubah (marriage contract), shown in plate 10.1, was written on pages torn out of an exercise book used at the time in Soviet schools. When many years later we applied for membership of one of the London synagogues we were asked to produce our ketubah. I am sure the administration of our synagogue in London had never seen such a ketubah, neither before, nor after.

After Israel's victory in 1967 young Jews became more interested in the Jewish religion and way of life and more courageous. More and more of them started to visit the famous Leningrad synagogue, celebrate Jewish holidays, especially Simchat Torah and Purim, and study Hebrew. Some of the young people who had never had any knowledge and experience of the Jewish way of life came to my parents and other observant Jews in order to observe how the Passover Seder was conducted. Before we left the Soviet Union in 1978, we were able to witness the revival of Jewish life in Leningrad.

11

Jewish Artists and Their Survival in the Soviet times

11(a) Yehuda Pen – Chagall's Teacher

Originally published in Jewish Renaissance,
vol. 7, issue 4, 2008, pp. 40-41

The 2008 exhibition 'From Russia' at the Royal Academy of Art attracted enormous interest, not least among the Jewish visitors. The review in the Jewish Chronicle (6 February) even had a heading 'Russian art? Jewish, more like'. So it is an appropriate moment to pay homage to a man who founded a Jewish Art School which produced many prominent painters of the 20th century, among them Chagall, Lissitzky, Yudovin and Zadkin, and was himself a great painter. His name is Yehuda Pen (1854-1937).

Yehuda (Yuri) Moiseevich Pen was born in 1854 to an Orthodox Jewish family. His love of art persuaded him to apply to the Imperial Academy of Art in St. Petersburg. His application was unsuccessful, and he lived illegally in St. Petersburg for a year, practising drawing at the Hermitage museum, before being admitted to the Academy on his second attempt. After finishing his studies in 1886, he moved to Vitebsk in Belarus where 60% of residents were Jews.

Vitebsk (a provincial capital) later gained international fame thanks to the paintings of Marc Chagall. Pen lived there until his death and created major works of art which made him famous. Among these were 'The Shadchen' (Matchmaker); 'The Maggid' (Preacher); 'The Glazier'; 'The Tailor'; 'The Last Sabbath', 'A letter from America', 'A praying Jew with the Torah', and many others.

In Pen's pictures the Jewish shtetl comes alive. A most interesting painting is 'The Get' (Divorce) depicting a session of a Rabbinic Court. The painting is open to several interpretations but is most likely the plea of a husband to the Court to grant a divorce on grounds of his wife's infertility.

In 1897 Pen opened a private Jewish School of Drawing and Painting in Vitebsk, the first in the Russian empire. The presence of such a teacher inspired local Jewish youth to enter the world of art and over the next two decades a steady stream of talented students, including Marc Chagall, passed through its doors.

To Pen, and his generation of Jewish artists in Russia, artistic activity was a means of Jewish national and spiritual revival. Pen's School functioned until 1918 when Chagall, who was appointed an Art Commissar of the Vitebsk province, opened the People's Art School and invited his teacher to head one of its studios. Later Pen became the School pro-rector and worked there until it was closed in 1923.

In 1921 a major exhibition in Vitebsk honoured the 25th anniversary of Pen's work in the city. Marc Chagall wrote to him:

> Dear Yuri Moiseevich, so Vitebsk, the city for which you have done so much, has, or will soon, celebrate your anniversary. For my part, I could not pass up the opportunity to send you these few lines. I remember as a child climbing the stairs to your studio. How I trembled, waiting for you – you were going to decide my fate. I know how many other Vitebsk natives' fates you also decided. For nearly a decade your studio, the city's first, beckoned. You were the first in Vitebsk. The city cannot forget you. You raised a great generation of Jewish artists. The Russian Jewish community should and will know about this. I am convinced that Vitebsk, to which you have given 25 years of your life, will sooner or later immortalise your labour as you so deserve. Your best works, which capture a particular kind of Russian and Jewish life, will be exhibited in a future Vitebsk city museum, while we, some of your students, will remember you with special fondness. No matter how far we may be separated from you in matters of art. Your image as an honourable artist toiler and first teacher looms forever large. I love you for it. My dear and first teacher, 1 embrace you on the occasion of your 25th anniversary – 25 years of service to Vitebsk. Live long and continue your beloved work.

Indeed, Chagall was Yehuda Pen's beloved pupil. This love shines through the famous portrait of young Chagall (1908).

In the 1920s and 30s some of Pen's pictures were shown at exhibitions in the Belarus capital, Minsk, and in Moscow. Nevertheless, in a letter to one of his friends he complained that being a Jewish artist, he would prefer to be exhibited as such but he doubted if most of his works would be accepted given their lack of revolutionary character.

In his last years, under the pressure of Stalin's regime, Pen was forced to produce pictures that complied with the ideological requirements of the time: 'Young Communist Shoemaker', 'The Proletarian Journalist' and others. Pen went on working in Vitebsk until he was murdered in his home in 1937, probably by a robber who thought (mistakenly) that his victim was a rich man.

In 1974, 1 had an opportunity to see Pen's pictures in Minsk. One of the curators from the National Art Museum of Belarus took the most important pictures from storage and organised a private viewing for me. He said jokingly that if the visitors to the museum knew what was being shown in that room they would all run there. He told me the story of the survival of the paintings during WW2. The German army captured Minsk on 28 June 1941 and Vitebsk on 11 July. The staff of the Minsk and Vitebsk museums understood that Pen's pictures would be destroyed if they fell into Nazi hands. Knowing their importance, they managed to pack them and send them to the Urals for safekeeping. Some did not even have time to flee themselves, sacrificing their lives for the sake of the paintings.

After the end of the War, all Pen's paintings, numbering more than 300, were entrusted to the National Art Museum in Minsk but most of them were put into storage for almost 50 years. Stalin's antisemitic policy meant that pictures of such explicitly Jewish character could not be shown.

Only after the collapse of the Soviet Union were Pen's pictures taken out of storage. Some were returned to the Vitebsk Art Museum, so eventually Chagall's prophecy was fulfilled. The authorities in Belarus are now happy to show Pen's pictures all over the world. In 1995 they were shown in the New York Jewish Museum as a part of the exhibition of Russian Jewish Artists. Perhaps it is the right time now to organise such an exhibition in London where the paintings of Yehuda Pen have never been seen.

11(b) Natan Altman - Surviving as a Soviet artist

Originally published in Jewish Renaissance,
vol. 8, issue 2, 2009, pp. 42-43

Among the most interesting pictures shown in the 2008 remarkable Royal Academy exhibition 'From Russia', were many created by Russian-Jewish painters. They included the famous portrait of the great Russian poetess, Anna Akhmatova, by Natan Altman. Few of Altman's other pictures have been exhibited in the West and his name is not widely known.

Natan Isaevich Altman was born in 1889 in the town of Vinnitsa. Ukraine. He was four years old when his father died of tuberculosis. His mother, tired by exhausting work and the constant concern of feeding the family, went abroad and Natan was left with his grandmother. They lived in great poverty in half a room, the second half rented to another big family. When Natan was 18, he managed to get into art school in Odessa, returning to Vinnitsa after four years to earn his living by giving drawing lessons. Meanwhile he started to paint pictures reflecting aspects of Jewish life. Among these are the portrait of his grandmother dressed in her best Saturday jacket and skirt (1908); The portrait of an old Jew (1910) and Jewish Funeral (1911) which reflects memories of the death of his grandfather.

When his grandmother died of cholera, Altman was left alone. He would have liked to have settled in St Petersburg but this was only permitted to Jews who were rich merchants, university-educated or artisans. It was easier to go to Paris where he arrived in 1910 to study for ten months. While he was there, two of his pictures were exhibited in one of the most prestigious art galleries and achieved immediate approval by French artists.

From the outset of his career, Altman was involved in most aspects of Jewish national expression. In Paris he became associated with a group of young Russian Jewish artists who called themselves Makhmadim ('precious' in Hebrew). They aspired to create a modern Jewish style by fusing Eastern European folk sources with the most contemporary West European artistic techniques. Altman quickly assimilated fauvism and cubism, combining them with an academic style depicting neutral subjects: portraits, still life and landscapes.

Back in Vinnitsa, in 1912, Altman obtained the qualification of a decorator which gave him the right to settle in St Petersburg. There he pursued his idea of creating a new Jewish art. He became interested in sculpture. The most interesting work of this period is *The Head of a Young Jew* in which he depicts himself with the chasidic side-curls. By this time Altman was already one of Russia's leading artists. In 1916 he was a founding member of the Jewish Society for the Encouragement of the Arts. This Society organised exhibitions and publications of modern Jewish art and promoted young Jewish artists, such as Altman, Chagall, Falk and Lissitzky, who, while aware of Jewish tradition, were seeking original directions that owed much to cubism and futurism.

Altman, like many Russian Jews, eagerly supported the Bolshevik *Revolution and the new government* and from 1918-21 he was a member of the Art Department of the Commissariat (Ministry) of Education. In 1920 he was invited to move to the State's new capital, Moscow, and commissioned to produce a series of drawings and bas-reliefs of Lenin to celebrate Lenin's 50th birthday. He was given a pass to the Kremlin and Lenin's office, where he went every day for six weeks, five to six hours a day, making sketches while Lenin worked in his office. In one sketch Lenin is depicted talking with representatives of the English Trade Unions. In 1921 the collected drawings were published under the title *Lenin. Drawings by Natan Altman*. He presented the first copy to Lenin. In the 1920s Altman worked for the State Jewish theatre and became friendly with its leading actor, and later chief director. Solomon Mikhoels, whose portrait he painted in 1927. In 1922 he made designs and decorations for *The Dybbuk* by S. An-sky the first production of the Habimah Hebrew theatre in Moscow (later to become the National Theatre of Israel).

In 1928 Altman accompanied the State Jewish Theatre on its European tour. The theatre returned to Moscow, but Altman stayed in Paris. Altman continued to send his pictures and drawings to exhibitions in Moscow and Leningrad, took part in exhibitions of Soviet art in Europe and the USA and sent drawings and articles to the Soviet newspapers. He designed the sets for a Soviet play about the Civil War in Russia staged by a pro-communist theatre in Paris. Altman avoided contact with Russian emigres. He considered himself a representative of Soviet culture and was outspoken in expressing dedication to his Motherland. In an article in *Literary Leningrad* of November 1935 he wrote:

"The situation in the West is such that art withers. Artistic Paris as well as the whole West is shaken by an economic crisis. Art is not needed by anyone now. I cannot think about subjects for my art now I am abroad. Only my Motherland, the USSR, can give me great topics."

He returned to the Soviet Union in 1936 and settled in Leningrad. There he worked mainly for the theatre and no longer addressed Jewish subjects. There were good reasons for this. 1936-38 and 1947-53 were the years of Stalin's purges and terror (the last wave of which was specifically directed against Jews) when many of Altman's friends and colleagues were arrested, shot or sent to labour camps. Among them were the famous theatre director Vsevolod Meyerhold, the writer Isaac Babel and the poet Osip Mandelstam. Solomon Mikhoels was killed in 1948 on the direct orders of Stalin, as described in Chapter 8. Their fate greatly affected Altman who lived in constant fear for his life. He was probably saved by some kind of immunity given by his drawings and sculptures of Lenin.

In 1969 I had the opportunity to attend a retrospective exhibition of Altman's work in Leningrad, held to mark his 80th birthday. Many admirers of Altman's art came from Moscow and other cities of the USSR to see this exhibition, a major event in the cultural life of the country. My brother, who accompanied me to the exhibition, brought with him several issues of a magazine published in Russia and USSR from 1916 to 1930 in which several drawings of Altman on Jewish topics were reproduced. (He had bought these in a second-hand book shop in Leningrad). By this time it was not dangerous to show, for example, a portrait of Solomon Mikhoels, whose name became kosher after the death of Stalin in March 1953 and who was remembered again as a great actor and director. Altman mingled with the visitors and readily answered their questions. My brother approached him and asked why no pictures of Jewish subjects were exhibited. He also tried to show Altman the drawings in the magazines he had brought with him. When Altman heard his questions, he became visibly scared and responded angrily: "I don't want to see these magazines". He immediately fled to the other end of the room. I understood that even 16 years after Stalin's death, he could not forget the times of terror.

Natan Isaevich Altman died on 12 December 1970 in Leningrad. He was buried in the small cemetery in the suburban settlement Komarovo, next to Anna Akhmatova. They met again – the artist and his model.

11(c) Anatoly Kaplan – Artist from the Shtetl

Originally published in Jewish Renaissance,
vol. 8, issue 4, 2009, pp. 38-39

A major exhibition of 200 works of the Russian-Jewish artist Amatoli Kaplan took place in 2006 at the Mikhailovsky Castle branch of St. Petersburg's famous Russian Museum. This exhibition, mounted more than 25 years after the artist's death, was evidence of an increased interest in his creations.

Anatoly Kaplan was one of the last of the great artists to come from small shtetls in the Pale of Settlement of the Russian Empire. Unlike the Russian artists featured in previous *Jewish Renaissance* articles – Marc Chagall, Yehuda Pen (see 11(a)) and Natan Altman (see 11(b) here) – Kaplan was not a part of any organisation or Jewish group and had practically no connection with his Jewish colleagues. At the same time he considered it his duty to preserve the Jewish shtetl and its inhabitants for the future generations. Nostalgia for his youth in a provincial town in Belarus created indelible impressions that inspired Kaplan's art throughout his life.

Anatoly (Tankhum) Lvovich Kaplan was born in 1902 in Rogachev (a shtetl in Belarus) to a family of a butcher with modest earnings and many children. His artistic abilities were evident very early. Together with his childhood friend, Samuil Galkin, (a future well-known poet), he used to make signs for local shoemakers. After the Bolshevik Revolution in 1917, Kaplan moved to Leningrad where he studied at the famous Academy of Arts. In the 1930s, he studied the art of lithography in the workshop of the Leningrad Artists' Union under the great Russian graphic artist G S Vereisky and very soon became a fervent enthusiast of this genre. Kaplan always remembered Vereisky with great warmth and gratitude and considered him as his real teacher. For his part, Vereisky greatly admired Kaplan 's art and gave him strong moral support. The superb portrait of Kaplan by Vereisky in 1958 is evidence of the deep mutual empathy of these artists.

In 1937 Kaplan was commissioned by the State Ethnographic Museum in Leningrad to create a series of lithographs depicting life in the Jewish Autonomous Region of Birobidzhan. In the late 1930s, Kaplan showed his dedication to Jewish subjects by creating the first of an extensive series of

illustrations of the stories of the great Yiddish writer Sholem Aleichem
which he continued throughout his life. His graphics series, *Kasrilevka*
(based on the name of a fictional Jewish shtletl from the books of Sholem
Aleichem) drew its inspiration from nostalgic recollections of his native
town of Rogachev. On his return to Leningrad in 1944, after evacuation to
the Urals during World War II, Kaplan made expressive lithographs that
provide a unique portrait of Leningrad in the aftermath of the German
siege, as well as the rebuilding that followed.

In 1947 Stalin launched an anti-Jewish campaign which continued until
his death in 1953. It was dangerous to work on Jewish topics in the
atmosphere of fear and terror. In order to survive this terrible time, Kaplan
found work at the Lomonosov porcelain factory which allowed him to
provide for his family and gave him some protection. The most prominent
Jewish writers and actors were shot in 1952 or sent to the labour camps. In
1950 Kaplan's childhood friend Samuil Galkin was arrested and sent to a
labour camp in the North (miraculously he survived and was released in
1955). After Stalin's death, during the so-called 'thaw', Kaplan resumed his
illustrations to the stories of Sholem Aleichem but he was still fearful and
exercised extreme caution.

Kaplan lived in a communal flat (a Soviet creation – a large flat
occupied by multiple families, sharing toilet and kitchen facilities). When
drawing, he would pin his paper to the door which opened into his room.
Nosey neighbours dropping in would not be able to see the subject of his
drawings. By the end of 1957 Kaplan understood the importance of his new
works but knew that powerful support would be needed to publish
drawings on Jewish topics. With this in mind, he approached the famous
Russian Jewish writer and journalist, Ilya Ehrenburg, President of the USSR-
France Friendship Society. With the help of Ehrenburg and his influential
friends, Kaplan's work became known outside the USSR and very soon he
achieved international recognition and subsequently success even in his
own country. Moreover, when at the end of 1950s, the Soviet government
wanted to show that Jewish art was flourishing in the USSR, they sent
Kaplan's works to international exhibitions in France, Italy, Austria, East
Germany, Canada, USA and other countries.

In 1959 the whole world celebrated the 100th anniversary of the birth
of Sholem Aleichem. The Soviet authorities permitted the publication of
the collected works of Sholem Aleichem in six volumes but they refused to
allow Kaplan to include his illustrations. During 1953-63 Kaplan had
created an extensive series of colour lithographs on the theme of Sholem
Aleichem's story 'The Bewitched Tailor'. An album containing these

lithographs was published but could be sold abroad only after special permission was given by the Central Committee of the Soviet Communist Party and the Ministry of Culture of the USSR. In 1961 Kaplan's works were exhibited in London in the Grosvenor Gallery. He received awards in France, Italy and East Germany. Kaplan's lithographs were shown in 25 countries but he was never allowed to travel abroad.

In 1967, Sholem Aleichem's *Tevye the Milkman* with Kaplan's lithographs was published in East Germany. Kaplan continued to work on graphic renditions of stories by Sholem Aleichem, with whose work he felt a spiritual affinity, as he did for all themes from Jewish songs and folk tales. His lithographs for *The Bewitched Tailor, The Song of Songs, Stempenu, Stories for Children* and *Tevye the Milkman* are nostalgic renderings of the shtetl life, and exhibit a profound understanding of the Jewish soul, character and sympathy with ordinary people.

In his lithographs, Kaplan employed various techniques to create rich surfaces and gradations of light and shade. He also experimented with materials and approaches to application, in order to create diverse, rich effects. In his later graphic work he introduced intense colours and dominant shapes just as he did in his still life paintings, ceramic reliefs and small-scale sculptures, often reworking motifs from his Jewish illustrations. As an artist whose work recaptures a century old folk-art culture, Kaplan's rendition offers a link with a vanished tradition.

Kaplan died in 1980. After the collapse of the USSR it became possible to exhibit his works outside Russia without any hindrance by the authorities. For example, his works were shown in 1991 at the extensive exhibition ' Russian Jewish Art' at the Royal College of Art, London, and in 1995 at the exhibition 'Russian Jewish Artists in a Century of Change', at the Jewish Museum in New York. A retrospective exhibition of Kaplan's works was held at the State Russian Museum, St Petersburg in 1995. The increased interest in Kaplan's works, the availability of many unknown works and this year's 150th anniversary of the birth of Sholem Aleichem might be the appropriate opportunity to organise an exhibition in London.